preserves

preserves

the complete book of jams, jellies,
pickles, relishes and chutneys,
with over 150 stunning recipes

Catherine Atkinson
& Maggie Mayhew

LORENZ BOOKS

This edition is published by Lorenz Books

Lorenz Books is an imprint of Anness Publishing Ltd
Hermes House, 88–89 Blackfriars Road, London SE1 8HA
tel. 020 7401 2077; fax 020 7633 9499
www.lorenzbooks.com; info@anness.com

UK agent: The Manning Partnership Ltd, 6 The Old Dairy, Melcombe Road,
Bath BA2 3LR; tel. 01225 478 444; fax 01225 478 440
sales@manning-partnership.co.uk

UK distributor: Grantham Book Services Ltd, Isaac Newton Way,
Alma Park Industrial Estate, Grantham, Lincs NG31 9SD; tel. 301 459 3366
fax 01476 541061; orders@gbs.tbs-ltd.co.uk

North American agent/distributor: National Book Network, 4501 Forbes
Boulevard, Suite 200, Lanham, MD 20706; tel. 301 459 3366
fax 301 429 5746; www.nbnbooks.com

Australian agent/distributor: Pan Macmillan Australia, Level 18, St Martins
Tower, 31 Market St, Sydney, NSW 2000; tel. 1300 135 113
fax 1300 135 103; customer.service@macmillan.com.au

New Zealand agent/distributor: David Bateman Ltd, 30 Tarndale Grove,
Off Bush Road, Albany, Auckland; tel. (09) 415 7664; fax (09) 415 8892

A CIP catalogue record for this book is available from the British Library.

Publisher: Joanna Lorenz
Managing Editor: Linda Fraser
Senior Editor: Susannah Blake
Production Controller: Wanda Burrows
Photographer: Craig Robertson
Home Economist: Sarah O'Brien
Assistant Home Economist: Emma Robertson
Stylist: Helen Trent

10 9 8 7 6 5 4 3 2 1

NOTES

Bracketed terms are intended for American readers.

For all recipes, quantities are given in both metric and imperial measures
and, where appropriate, measures are also given in standard cups and spoons.
Follow one set, but not a mixture, because they are not interchangeable.
Standard spoon and cup measures are level.
1 tsp = 5ml, 1 tbsp = 15ml, 1 cup = 250ml/8fl oz
Australian standard tablespoons are 20ml. Australian readers should use
3 tsp in place of 1 tbsp for measuring small quantities of flour, salt, etc.

Medium (US large) eggs are used unless otherwise stated.

This book has been written with the reader's safety in mind, and the advice,
information and instructions are intended to be clear and safe to follow. However,
cooking with boiling hot mixtures can be dangerous and there is a risk of burns if
sufficient care is not taken. Neither the author nor the publisher can accept any
legal responsibility or liability for any errors or omissions made, or for accidents
in the kitchen.

contents

THE HISTORY OF PRESERVING

Preserving seasonal fruits and vegetables as jams, jellies, chutneys and relishes is one of the oldest of culinary arts. Once essential for basic survival, preserving is nowadays more often employed to store seasonal vegetables or fruits. It can be done in two ways: by heat sterilization, which destroys enzymes and bacteria, or by creating an environment where contaminants are unable to thrive – by drying, salting, or adding sugar, vinegar or alcohol.

AN AGE-OLD TECHNIQUE

Preserving was one of the earliest skills acquired by man, essential for survival during the cold, dark winter months when fresh food was scarce. Sun and wind were the first natural agents to be used: fruits and vegetables laid out in the hot sun or hung in the wind to dry were found to last longer than fresh produce and were lighter and easier to carry. In colder, damp climates, smoke and fire were used to hasten the drying process.

These discoveries meant that travelling to new territories became easier and new settlements were built where it was feasible for people to both grow and store food. It wasn't long before early man found that salt was a powerful dehydrator, far more consistent and reliable than the natural elements of sun and wind. Salt soon became a highly prized commodity – so much so that wars were fought over it. In fact, sometimes the salt was more valuable than the food it preserved, hence the saying that something is not worth its salt. Using salt to preserve foods made long-distance travel more possible because produce that had previously been perishable could be taken on board ships for journeys that lasted months and sometimes even years.

The preservative properties of vinegar and alcohol were discovered around the same time as those of salt, and people also realized that food could be flavoured at the same time that it was being preserved. Vinegar, which creates an acid environment that contaminants cannot live in, was used throughout the world. Malt vinegars were common in countries where beer was brewed, wine vinegar where vines were grown and rice vinegar became popular in the Far East.

Surprisingly the use of sugar as a preservative wasn't discovered until many centuries later. Cane sugar, brought to Europe by Arab merchants in the 12th century, remained a scarce luxury in the Western world for 400 years. It wasn't until the 16th century, when it was introduced to Europe from the West Indies, that sugar became a sought-after ingredient. Soon the demand for it became so great that it encouraged the rise of colonialism and the slave trade. In the 18th century, beetroot (beet), which had always been enjoyed as a vegetable, began to be cultivated specifically for its sugar content. Eventually sugar became plentiful and cheap, and the liking for sweet preserves started to grow.

It was during the 19th century that preserving really came into its own and was considered to be a skilled craft. Many of the recipes we use today are based on those that first appeared in cookbooks

Left: Rich, fruity chutneys were first made in India and became popular in Britain in the 19th century.

Above: Bottling fruits in flavoured syrups was one of the earliest ways that sugar was used for preserving.

during that era. Housewives took pride in filling capacious larders (pantries) with bottles and jars of preserves made from summer and autumn fruits while they were plentiful. These were then enjoyed during the lean winter months to supplement their diet, which would otherwise have consisted mainly of salted meats and root vegetables.

In the 20th century, preserving became less fashionable. Many homes had less storage space and, as the range and use of commercially prepared foods and preserves increased, huge stocks of home-made preserves were no longer needed or desirable. Imported produce meant that many fruits and vegetables were available all year round – soft fruits could be bought in the winter months and citrus fruits never disappeared from grocers' shelves. By the middle of the century, refrigerators could be found in most homes, followed by freezers in the 1960s and 70s, and during those decades freezing became the preferred way of preserving fruit and vegetables and the old-fashioned techniques became less popular.

PRESERVE-MAKING TODAY

Nowadays though, the art of preserving is coming back into its own, not because food needs to be processed to make it keep for long periods but for reasons of quality and variety. Improved travel and communication have increased knowledge of preserves from around the world and more unusual varieties of fruit, vegetables and flavouring ingredients are now readily available. Many people prefer to make their own preserves instead of buying mass-produced products with artificial flavourings and colourings. The satisfaction that comes from being able to create a unique product is also being rediscovered.

This book contains a comprehensive and detailed reference section showing how to make sweet and savoury preserves. All the main techniques are shown, including jam-, jelly- and marmalade-making; bottling fruits; pickling; chutney- and relish-making; candying; and drying. There is also a fabulous full-colour guide to the ingredients used for preserving – from seasonal fruits and vegetables to flavourings and preservatives.

The stunning recipe collection includes a whole host of traditional and contemporary ideas that will prove to be an inspiration and pleasure to both the novice jam-maker and the experienced preserver.

Below: Nowadays jams and conserves are made with a huge range of exotic ingredients.

SOFT FRUITS AND BERRIES

These delicate fruits are the epitome of summer and early autumn and can be made into wonderful jams and jellies. Despite their distinctive flavours and appearance, many are interchangeable in recipes. They can also be preserved in alcohol, but are less successful when bottled in syrup and are almost never included in pickles and chutneys. Soft berries are most often used in jams and conserves, while currants and cranberries are particularly good made into jellies.

STRAWBERRIES

These fruits are one of the most popular berries for jam-making and have a wonderfully fragrant flavour. Choose medium-size berries with an intense fragrance as these will give the preserve a good fruity flavour. Look for just-ripe, firm, fresh berries and use them for jam-making as soon as possible after picking, as this is when the

Below: Strawberries are one of the most popular fruits for jam-making.

Right: Raspberries can be made into intensely flavoured jams, jellies and conserves.

pectin content is highest. Rinse them only if absolutely necessary; if you do wash them, don't cut or hull them beforehand, or water will penetrate the fruit.

Tiny wild strawberries (*fraise de bois*), also known as alpine strawberries, have a pungent aroma and flavour and can be used whole in conserves.

THE RASPBERRY AND BLACKBERRY FAMILY

Technically, each berry is composed of multiple fruits as every tiny segment contains a hard seed. Jams made from these fruits have a high seed content, so they are often strained and made into seedless jams or jellies. The true raspberry is a bright crimson colour; yellow and white raspberries are also available and these have a deliciously delicate flavour, but make less attractive preserves.

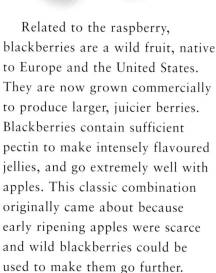

Related to the raspberry, blackberries are a wild fruit, native to Europe and the United States. They are now grown commercially to produce larger, juicier berries. Blackberries contain sufficient pectin to make intensely flavoured jellies, and go extremely well with apples. This classic combination originally came about because early ripening apples were scarce and wild blackberries could be used to make them go further.

Dewberries are closely related to the blackberry and are similar in appearance. Cloudberries, which grow in North America and Canada, are a bright orange-red colour; the Scandinavian (or Arctic) cloudberry, which also grows in Scotland, is a pinky yellow colour with an almost caramel flavour. Loganberries (a cross between the raspberry and the Pacific blackberry) look like elongated, very dark raspberries but have a juicier, fuller flavour. Tayberries are a similar hybrid and are large, conical and deep purple. Boysenberries are long, dark red berries with a sharp flavour. All these berries can be successfully preserved in the same way as raspberries and blackberries.

CURRANTS

Black-, red- and whitecurrants have a sharp, intense flavour and are picked in bunches on stems. Blackcurrants and redcurrants are most common; whitecurrants are an albino strain of redcurrants and have a less acidic flavour. High in both pectin and acid, currants need little cooking. Blackcurrants are usually made into jam, and red- and whitecurrants into jelly.

The simplest way to remove currants from the stalk is to run the prongs of a fork gently down the stalk over a bowl.

BLUEBERRIES AND BILBERRIES

Blueberries and bilberries are small, dark fruits that grow wild in Britain, Europe and the United States. Bilberries, the European species, are dark bluish black with a soft bloom. The slightly flattened sphere-shaped berries measure no more than 1cm/½in across. The larger cultivated blueberry and the wild huckleberry have a similar appearance but a sweeter flavour.

Below: Blueberries have a mild, fragrant flavour and can be made into richly coloured jams.

CRANBERRIES

Small, hard, shiny, deep red cranberries are a member of the blueberry and bilberry family. They are much too sour to eat raw but, once cooked with sugar, can be transformed into sparkling bright red jellies and rich, jam-like sauces, which are traditionally served with turkey.

GOOSEBERRIES

Popular in northern Europe, gooseberries are rarely eaten in other parts of the world. Most bushes produce hard oval berries, dark green in colour with paler stripes, and a smooth or, more usually, fuzzy skin. There is also a softer, pale purple variety.

The fruit is usually too sour to eat raw, but can be made into jellies, jams, chutneys and relishes. Gooseberries are rich in pectin, especially when slightly unripe, so they produce jams and jellies with a good set. Unless the mixture is being strained or sieved, they should be "topped and tailed" (trimmed) before preserving.

PHYSALIS

Also known as Cape gooseberries, although they are unrelated to gooseberries. The golden berries are enclosed in an inedible papery husk. They make good, if rather expensive, jams and bottled fruits.

Above: Tiny redcurrants have a distinctive, tart flavour and are particularly good made into sparkling jellies.

HEDGEROW FRUITS

Elderberries are the fruit of elderberry trees, which grow all over Europe and West Asia and the United States. The berries are small and very dark bluish black and hang in umbrella-like clusters. They can be stripped from the sprigs with a fork and are excellent preserved with crab apples or cooking apples.

Haws are the small dark berries of the hawthorn or May tree. They are slightly astringent and very good cooked with apples to make a dark red jelly.

Hips or rosehips are the orangey red seedpods of the rose and can be made into a bittersweet jelly.

Sloes, a type of plum, are the fruit of the blackthorn bush, which is found in Europe and West Asia. The fruits are black with a blue bloom, and measure only about 1cm/½in across. They can be combined with apples and made into a fragrant jelly.

ORCHARD FRUITS

Apples and pears, which are available all year round, are the most common members of this family of fruits. They can be made into jams, jellies and chutneys, bottled in syrup or dried into chewy rings. Other, more unusual, orchard fruits include quinces, japonicas and medlars.

APPLES

There are thousands of varieties of apples, although choice in the shops is usually limited to just a few. Among the most popular eating apples are Gala, Russet, Granny Smith, Braeburn, Golden Delicious and Cox's Orange

Below: Apples are used in almost every type of preserve – from sweet jellies to spicy relishes.

Above: Pears are equally good bottled in sweet syrups or spiced vinegars and make a tasty addition to sweet-and-sour chutneys.

Pippin. These all have their own individual flavours that are captured when the apples are bottled in spiced or flavoured syrup. Well-flavoured eating apples may also be used in chutneys and relishes when retaining the texture of the fruit is desirable. Cooking apples are more frequently used in preserves and give a good pulpy texture to chutneys.

Apples are high in pectin and, on their own, produce rather bland, colourless jams. They are therefore often combined with fruits with a good flavour and low pectin content to produce a jam or jelly with a better set. Using apples as a base is also a good way to make expensive fruit go further. Mild-flavoured apple jelly makes a good base for herb jellies. The jelly usually takes on a pinkish colour, so traditionally a few drops of green food colouring are added.

Most of the pectin in apples is found in the skin and seeds so apple peelings and cores are often used to make a pectin stock. This is then stirred into other fruit jams and jellies to improve their set, without affecting their flavour.

CRAB APPLES

These small apples can be gathered from the wild, from cultivated garden trees or, very occasionally, bought from independent food stores. They have a sharp, rich flavour and are very good used on their own or combined with other hedgerow fruit.

CORING APPLES AND PEARS

To core apples, place a corer over the stalk end and push it right through the fruit. Gently twist the corer and carefully pull out the core.
To core pears, start at the base of the fruit and push the corer only half way through.

To remove the core from halved fruit, scoop out the cores using a melon baller or a teaspoon to make a neat round hole.

PEARS

Unlike apples,
pears are low in
pectin, so are less frequently used
in jams and jellies. Their sweet,
mild flavour and tender texture
makes them popular for chutney-
making and they are superb
preserved in syrup or alcohol, or
pickled in raspberry vinegar, either
whole, halved or quartered. Pears
are divided into eating and cooking
varieties, although some eating
pears are also suitable for cooking.
The British Conference and the
American Bosc are particularly
good for preserving.

QUINCES

Golden yellow quinces can be the
shape and size of a small squat
pear or a small apple, or as large
as big pears, depending on the
variety. The flesh is hard,
granular and sour when
eaten raw, but cooking
makes it smooth and

tender, with a
delicate tinged soft
pink colour and a sherbet-like
aromatic flavour. Quinces are rich in
pectin and they can be made into
jellies, fruit cheeses and butters;
these may be a rich golden or a
deep pink colour depending on the
variety of quince used.

JAPONICAS

These small, round, green fruits
are also known as Japanese
quinces. They can be preserved
in the same ways as quinces,
but have a slightly sharper,
lemony flavour.

*Above: Medlars are not
widely available but, if you
can find them, they can be made
into really delicious preserves.*

MEDLARS

Medlars are small brown fruit with
a squashed round shape and an
open end revealing the seeds.
The flesh is very hard and mouth-
puckeringly acidic when first
picked. To soften and sweeten the
fruit, it must be "bletted" or
allowed to ferment slightly. The
flesh is dry and sticky and
tastes a little like the flesh
of dried dates. A mixture of
unripe and "bletted"
medlars can be made into
aromatic preserves such
as jams, jellies and
cheeses.

*Above: Quinces have a distinctive,
aromatic flavour and can be made
into delicious jellies, which are
good spread on bread or toast.*

STONE FRUITS

These are all fruits of the *prunus* genus, recognized by their single central woody stone (pit), soft flesh and thin skin. They are well-suited to jam-making and can also be used whole or halved in bottled preserves. These fruits come in a wide variety of colours, textures and flavours, from tender pale orange apricots and yellow-skinned tart plums, to glossy sweet red cherries, and they can be made into numerous types of preserves. Plums are available all year round, and although cherries, apricots, peaches and nectarines are sometimes available at other times of the year, they are at their peak in summer and early autumn.

PLUMS

These fruits range in colour from pale gold through red and crimson to deep purple. When buying, choose firm, unwrinkled fruit, which still have a slight bloom. They will keep for several days at room temperature, but will

Below: Plums are most plentiful in the summer, so it is well worth making a batch of jam to enjoy during the rest of the year.

Above: Sweet black cherries can be made into the most delicious, richly flavoured preserves.

continue to ripen. Once they are almost ripe, they can be stored in the refrigerator for a few more days. Use them when just-ripe to make richly flavoured jams.

Mirabelle plums are a French speciality, grown particularly around Alsace. They are small, round, red-flushed yellow plums with a powerful sweet scent. They are usually preserved whole in a liqueur-enriched syrup. Greengages are small, green, fragrant plums, primarily dessert fruits, but excellent bottled or made into luxurious jams.

Purple-black damsons are available only in the early autumn months. Small and sour-tasting, they make superb jams and damson cheese. Bullaces are small, round plums that grow wild throughout Europe and can be used in the same way as damsons.

CHERRIES

These fruits are divided into two main groups: sweet cherries, which may be black (actually deep red) or white (usually yellow), and sour cherries, of which the best known are Morellos. When buying, the cherry's stem is a good indicator of freshness – it should be green and flexible not brown and brittle. Avoid any fruit that is overly soft or split. Cherries are low in pectin, so must either be combined with apples or other pectin-rich fruit, or commercial or home-made pectin stock needs to be added when making jam or other set preserves. Both sweet and sour cherries are excellent pickled or bottled.

Below: Ripe, juicy peaches are delicious preserved in sweet syrups, spirits and liqueurs.

STONING FRUITS

Large stone fruits such as peaches, nectarines, plums and apricots can all be stoned (pitted) in the same way. Cherries can also be stoned in this way, but because they are so small, it is much easier to use a special cherry stoner.

1 Using a sharp knife, carefully cut around the middle of the fruit through the crease that runs from the stem to the tip, right through to the stone.

2 Twist the halves in opposite directions to separate; the stone will remain in one of the halves.

3 To remove the stone, carefully lever it out of the fruit with a knife.

Stoning cherries To remove the stones from cherries, use a cherry stoner. Pull the stalk from the cherry, then place the fruit in the cup of the stoner and squeeze the handles of the tool together. The short prong will push through the fruit and force out the stone.

SKINNING STONE FRUITS

1 Raw peaches, nectarines and thick-skinned plums are difficult to peel with a knife. To loosen the skins, put the fruits in a heatproof bowl and pour over enough boiling water to cover.

2 Leave to stand for 1 minute, then drain and cool the fruit under cold running water. The skin should now come off easily, using the point of a small knife to peel it away.

PEACHES AND NECTARINES

A good peach or nectarine will be richly coloured and heavy, with a strong aroma. Peaches have downy skins and the most common types have yellow or pink flesh. The white-fleshed and pale-skinned variety is the sweetest of all.

Nectarines are similar to peaches but they have smooth and shiny skins and a slightly sharper taste – like a cross between a peach and a plum. They make great jams, are good pickled or bottled, and are also excellent made into fruity chutneys. Peaches and nectarines should be skinned when making jams and chutneys.

APRICOTS

With their slightly sweet-and-sour flavour, soft texture and downy skins, apricots are delicious eaten fresh and raw. Cooking with sugar intensifies their flavour. Slightly under-ripe apricots can be poached in a sugar syrup with a dash of lime juice and bottled. Just-ripe fruit can be cooked with sugar to make jams.

Right: Smooth-skinned nectarines can be preserved in the same way as peaches.

Apricots and almonds are a very popular combination and split almonds can be added to special conserves for extra flavour and texture. When choosing apricots, pick those with the strongest colour for the sweetest flavour.

CITRUS FRUITS

With their aromatic acidity, citrus fruits are the main ingredient of nearly all marmalades and fruit curds. They are also often added to other preserves because they have a high pectin and acid content, and they are frequently used in jams and jellies to help achieve a good set. Their pungency and sharpness adds not only flavour but also offsets sweetness. Members of the citrus family include lemons, limes, oranges, grapefruit and tangerines as well as the more exotic Ugli fruit, citrons and kumquats, and hybrids such as the clementine and limequat. All are covered in a thick peel, which consists mainly of white pith and a colourful outer layer of zest or rind.

Below: Sweet, juicy oranges are most commonly preserved as tangy breakfast marmalades.

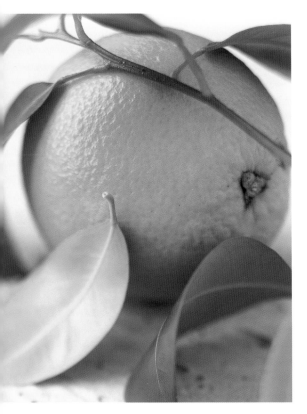

ORANGES

There are three types of sweet oranges: the common orange is a medium-size fruit with a fine-grained skin, and popular varieties are Valencia, Jaffa and Shamouti, which is available only in the winter. These are the juiciest oranges and are ideal for sweet marmalades and orange curds. They often contain a lot of pips (seeds), which are essential for marmalade-making because they are high in pectin.

Navel oranges are seedless, so are better preserved whole, in segments or in slices. Red-flushed blood oranges have ruby-coloured flesh and a rich, almost berry-like flavour. These make excellent marmalade when combined with sharper lemons, but are less successful for curd-making because their deeply coloured juice looks rather unappetizing when mixed with yellow butter and eggs.

Bitter Seville oranges have a high pectin and acid content, as well as an excellent, punchy flavour and make the finest marmalades. (The bulk of the Spanish crop is exported to Britain for this purpose.) The season is a fairly short one and they are only available for a few weeks during the winter. However, bitter oranges can be successfully frozen whole or chopped. Alternatively, the oranges can be chopped and cooked without sugar until very soft before cooling and freezing. When ready to use, they can be thawed and then boiled with sugar to setting point.

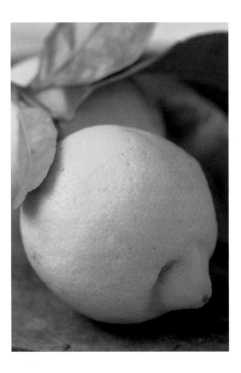

Above: Sharp, zesty lemons are widely used in both sweet and savoury preserves.

LEMONS

In the preserving kitchen, lemons are indispensable. They add acid and pectin to jams and jellies made from low-pectin fruit such as strawberries and peaches, which are difficult to set. Adding lemon juice to jellies also gives them a sparkling appearance. A dash of lemon juice added to preserves made from soft fruit such as strawberries and exotic fruits such as papayas, helps bring out their flavour. A few spoonfuls of lemon juice added to cold water makes an acidulated dip that will prevent cut fruit such as pears and apples from discolouring.

Small, thin-skinned lemons are juicier, so are perfect for making curds; bigger, more knobbly ones have a higher proportion of peel and pith to flesh, so are better for marmalades and candying.

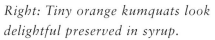
Right: Tiny orange kumquats look delightful preserved in syrup.

Above: Limes have a distinctive, sharp flavour and are equally delicious made into sweet marmalades and salty pickles.

LIMES

These small green fruits flourish in near-tropical conditions. They have a distinctive, tangy flavour and are one of the most sour citrus fruits. A squeeze of lime juice can be added to jams and jellies instead of lemon juice to enhance the flavour of the fruit and to improve the set. It goes particularly well with tropical fruits, such as mangoes and papayas.

GRAPEFRUITS

One of the largest citrus fruits, with a diameter of up to 15cm/6in. The flesh of grapefruits varies in colour from pale yellow to the dark reddish pink of sweeter ruby grapefruit. The yellow skinned and fleshed varieties have a sharp and refreshing flavour that makes good marmalade. Sweetie grapefruits are a less sharp variety with a vibrant bright green skin.

CITRONS

This large, lemon-shaped fruit grows to 20cm/8in in length. It has a fairly thick lumpy greenish yellow peel that is often candied and is used in commercial candied peel. The very sour-tasting pulp is sometimes made into sweet preserves, but it has no other culinary use.

POMELOS

Also known as the shaddock, this large citrus fruit resembles a pear-shaped grapefruit. The flesh can be used to make jams and the rind can be candied with sugar or used to make marmalade.

Left: Pink grapefruits have a milder flavour than yellow ones and can be made into very pretty preserves.

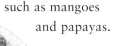

TANGERINES AND MANDARIN ORANGES

These are the generic names for small, flat citrus fruits with loose skins and a sweet or tart-sweet flavour. Satsumas, clementines and mineolas also fall into this group. Satsumas are slightly tart and very juicy; clementines (a cross between the tangerine and the bitter orange) are similar but have a thinner, more tight-fitting skin. Both fruits are almost seedless so are the best choice for preserving whole in sugar syrup. Mineolas are larger. They are hybrids of the grapefruit and tangerine, have a sharp, tangy flavour and resemble oranges in size and colour.

KUMQUATS AND LIMEQUATS

The tiny, orange, oval kumquat with its distinctive sweet-sour flavour can be eaten whole and unpeeled; the rind has a sweeter flavour than the flesh. Kumquats are delicious pickled, preserved in syrup or candied.

Limequats are a cross between a lime and a kumquat. The small, bright green fruits have a fragrant flavour and can be preserved in the same way as kumquats, although they have a slightly more sour flavour. The two fruits look very pretty bottled together in the same jar and make a lovely gift.

HYBRID FRUITS

There are a huge number of citrus hybrids that are bred for flavour, colour or to be seedless.

ugli fruit

Available in winter, this hybrid of the grapefruit, tangerine and orange has a loose, rough, greeny yellow skin and a slightly squashed appearance. It is very juicy and sweet and can be used instead of grapefruit in marmalades. The peel is very good candied.

temple oranges

These loose-skinned fruits are a cross between a tangerine and an orange. Slightly oval in shape, they have rough, thick, deep orange skin, which makes them popular for marmalade-making in the United States. The flesh is sweet, yet tart and contains a fair number of seeds. Temple oranges are in season from December to March.

buying and storing

Look for firm, plump citrus fruits that feel heavy for their size as this indicates that the fruit will be juicy. Avoid dry, wrinkled specimens, soft squashy fruit or any with brown spots. Green patches on lemons and yellow patches on limes are a sign of immaturity.

Citrus fruits can be kept at room temperature for several days, but for longer storage, keep them in the refrigerator, putting unwaxed fruit in a plastic bag. Always wash and scrub citrus fruits before using them in preserves.

GRATING CITRUS RIND
To make long, thin shreds, scrape a canelle knife or zester along the surface of the fruit, applying firm pressure.

To make finer shreds, gently rub the fruit over the fine side of a grater to remove the rind without taking off any bitter white pith. Use a dry pastry brush to brush off any rind that sticks to the grater.

CUTTING RIND INTO FINE STRIPS OR JULIENNE

1 Using a vegetable peeler or a sharp knife, remove strips of rind as thinly as possible, without taking off any of the bitter white pith.

2 Stack several strips of rind on top of each other and, using a sharp knife, cut them into fine strips or julienne.

FLAVOURING SUGAR
To add a hint of citrus flavour to a preserve, rub the fruit's skin with 1 or 2 sugar cubes, turning the cubes as each side becomes saturated with the oil. Weigh the cubes with the sugar.

PEELING CITRUS FRUIT
1 To peel large citrus fruit such as grapefruit, cut a slice from the top and bottom of the fruit, through the flesh, then cut away the rind, pith and skin, working from top to base, following the curve of the fruit.

2 To peel smaller fruits such as oranges, cut off the rind, pith and skin in a long spiral.

SEGMENTING CITRUS FRUIT
1 Holding the peeled fruit in one hand and the knife in the other, slice the knife down one side of a segment, cutting it away from the membrane. Cut down the other side and pull out the segment.

2 Repeat with the remaining segments, turning back the flaps of membrane like a book. When all the segments are removed, squeeze the remaining fruit to extract the juice.

TROPICAL FRUITS

With imports from many parts of the world, tropical fruits are now available all year round, but tend to be at their best during the winter months. They are often vibrantly coloured with fabulous flavours and make fragrant jams and luxurious chutneys.

PINEAPPLES

This distinctive fruit has extremely juicy, sweet and refreshing golden flesh. It can be made into lovely jams and crisp-textured relishes, which are ideal for serving with chicken, pork and ham. Pineapple rings are also good candied.

Once picked, pineapples do not ripen so always buy ripe fruits. (If you do buy an unripe fruit, leaving it for a few days may help reduce the acidity.) Ripe fruits should give off a sweet aroma and be orange all over with no brown parts. They can be stored in a cool place for up to a week.

PREPARING A PINEAPPLE

1 Using a sharp knife, slice off the base and plume of the pineapple. Rest the cut base on a board. Cut away the peel thinly, working from the top downwards, then cut out the "eyes" following their spiral around the fruit.

2 To make pineapple rings, cut the peeled fruit into thick slices, then remove the central core from each slice using a 2cm/¾in round cookie cutter.

GUAVAS

These fruits have a sweet, almost spicy aroma and flavour, with granular flesh that becomes creamy when ripe. The small oval fruits, no larger than 7.5cm/3in long, have a number of small seeds in the centre. Buy fruits with smooth skins and no wrinkling or brown patches around the stalk. Guavas will keep for a few days in the refrigerator but always wrap them in clear film (plastic wrap) because their aroma will permeate other foods. Peel them thinly, then halve and remove the seeds. They can be made into fragrant jams, cheeses and sparkling jellies, with a honey-like aroma, and pink or gold colour, depending on the variety used. It is essential to add lemon or lime juice to preserves that are made with guavas to achieve a good set and to heighten the flavour.

PAPAYAS

Also known as pawpaw, these pear-shaped fruits have a green skin that turns a speckled yellow when the fruit is ripe. The creamy textured flesh is a vibrant orange-pink colour with a wonderful sweet flavour and lovely perfumed aroma. To prepare papayas, cut them in half lengthways and scoop out the numerous black seeds. Use ripe fruits to make jams and butters, and firm, slightly under-ripe fruits to make chutneys.

Right: Pineapples have a sweet, sharp, tangy flavour and are good in jellies, jams and tangy relishes.

MANGOES

The skins of these luscious fruits range in colour from green, through yellow and orange to red. Ripe fruits have deep-orange flesh, which will yield slightly when the uncut fruit is gently squeezed. Just-ripe and green under-ripe mangoes can be made into excellent, highly flavoured chutneys and pickles, but over-ripe fruit should be avoided as mangoes tend to become more fibrous when very ripe and soft. When mangoes are scarce or expensive, substitute up to half the total weight of mangoes with cooking apples.

BANANAS

These long, yellow fruits make delicious, though not particularly attractive, jams. Their sweet flavour and soft, pulpy texture combine well with dried fruits such as dates and figs, which need a relatively short cooking time. They are also good in fruity chutneys,

PREPARING A MANGO

The simplest way to prepare a mango is to remove the skin with a vegetable peeler and slice the flesh off the stone (pit). To cut mango flesh into cubes, use the following method.

1 Hold the mango with one hand and cut vertically down one side of the stone. Repeat on the other side.

2 Cut into the flesh, but not all the way through the peel, lengthways and widthways.

3 Holding the mango slices with the flesh side upwards, press each slice inside out, opening the cuts in the flesh. Cut the mango cubes from the peel. Cut any remaining flesh from the stone, remove the peel and cube.

particularly spicy Indian-style preserves. It is best to use just-ripe bananas for preserves; choose ones with smooth, yellow skins that have only a few brown speckles.

Dried bananas are sun-dried in their skins, then peeled to reveal dark, sticky fruit inside. They have a concentrated flavour and can add sweetness to chutneys. Do not confuse them with banana chips, which are hard, dried slices of banana, unsuitable for preserving.

Below: Fragrant mangoes are fabulous made into sweet and tangy chutney.

Plantains, another member of the banana family, are "cooking" bananas. Green-skinned with flecks of brown, turning black when fully ripe, they may retain much of their shape after cooking and are good in vegetable chutneys.

Above: Although not traditionally throught of as a preserving fruit, bananas can be made into surprisingly good chutneys.

Left: Kiwi fruits can be made into pale green jams and chutneys.

POMEGRANATES

The shape and size of an orange, pomegranates have tough, leathery skin and a large calyx, and range in colour from deep yellow to crimson. Inside are dozens of white seeds surrounded by transluscent pinkish-red flesh, encased in a cream-coloured membrane. The seeds, pith and membranes are bitter so it is the juice that is extracted to make jams and jellies. The simplest way to do this is to cut the fruit in half and use a lemon squeezer to squeeze out the juice, taking care not to crush the seeds. Grenadine, a sweet syrup used in cocktails and mixed drinks, is made from pomegranate juice, and a dash of this can be used to flavour preserves.

Below: The bright pink flesh of pomegranates can be made into beautiful glistening jellies.

KIWI FRUITS

Although completely unrelated to the gooseberry, these fuzzy, brown, egg-shaped fruits were once known as Chinese gooseberries. The flesh is bright green with a sunray pattern of black seeds. Just-ripe fruit (when it yields to gentle pressure) should be used for jam-making. Kiwi fruit has a slightly sharp flavour so it is usually better to use sugar with pectin than to add lemon juice to get a good set.

PASSION FRUITS

These oval fruits have leathery reddish purple skins that become dimpled when the fruit is ripe. Inside are small, hard edible seeds, surrounded by fragrant, intensely flavoured orange pulp. The pulp and seeds may be scooped out of halved passion fruit shells and made into jam. Alternatively, the pulp can be rubbed through a fine sieve with a spoonful of boiling water to extract the juice, leaving the seeds behind. The juice can then be used with other fruit to make intensely flavoured, aromatic jams, jellies and curds.

Grenadillas are a larger, but less fragrant, member of this fruit family.

PERSIMMONS AND SHARON FRUIT

Rather like squarish, squashed tomatoes in shape, persimmons have a deep orange, smooth and shiny skin, and are about 6cm/2½in in diameter. Before they are ripe, the flesh has an astringent taste and pithy texture. The fruits tend to ripen suddenly, transforming into a soft, sweet fruit with no trace of bitterness. This quality encouraged the growers to develop the Sharon fruit, a golden-orange persimmon that is almost entirely seedless and sweet even when firm. The skins are tough, so the fruit should be peeled before making into jam, but this is not necessary when making jellies.

TAMARILLOS

This egg-shaped fruit of the tomato family (sometimes known as a "tree tomato"), may be yellow, red, or dark red; the yellow variety has the finest flavour. Tamarillos can be used in the same way as tomatoes to make pickles and chutneys, but the skin has a very bitter taste so the fruit should be peeled; blanch the fruits first to loosen their skins. Tamarillos can also be made into sweet jellies.

MELONS, GRAPES, DATES AND FIGS

These fruits don't fit into any particular category. They were among the first to be cultivated and all come in a vast array of shapes, sizes and colours.

MELONS

There are two kinds of melon: the dessert melon and the watermelon. Dessert melons may have green or yellow skins, sometimes streaky or netted (with fibrous markings), and fragrant, dense flesh, ranging from pale green to deep orange. Most are ripe if they yield under your thumb when pressed on the stem end. They should also give off a sweet aroma. Once ripe, they should be kept in a cool place and used within a few days. When cut they will keep for a day or two in the refrigerator. The flavour of melon in preserves is not intense. They work well if combined with strong flavourings such as ginger, or other fruits such as pineapple, passion fruit, peach and mango. They are also good scooped into balls with a melon baller or cut into cubes and pickled. Watermelons have a high water content, at around 90 per cent, so the flesh is rarely used in preserves. The skin though, can be diced and pickled.

GRAPES

Of the many grape varieties that are available, the smaller seedless grapes are preferable for preserves as they need less preparation and have thin skins with little tannin. Usually, grapes are referred to as either black or white, although the colours vary a great deal from pale green to pinkish red and dark purplish black. Grape flavours range from honey-sweet to sharp and almost lemon-scented. When buying, choose fruits that are firm with smooth skin and no sign of turning brown near the stem end. Store them in the refrigerator and bring to room temperature before using. Grapes make good jams, conserves and jellies that are sometimes flavoured with alcohol such as wine. They can also be pickled or included in chutneys and relishes.

Above: Juicy black grapes are good for making into delicate, fragrant, sparkling jellies.

Left: The orange flesh of cantaloupes is excellent scooped into balls and preserved in a sweet syrup.

RHUBARB
Technically, rhubarb is the stem of a vegetable. Outdoor-grown rhubarb is available in late spring and has crimson and green stems; forced rhubarb, cultivated indoors without light, has thin, tender, pale stems. The former can be made into chutney, the latter into a delicately flavoured jam. Rhubarb has a very sharp, intense flavour and goes particularly well with orange and ginger.

Above: Naturally sweet dates make the perfect addition to tangy sweet-and-sour chutneys.

DATES

Plump and glossy, fresh dates are soft and packed with concentrated sugar. The thin papery skins should be slipped off and the long stone (pit) removed before the flesh is added to chutneys. When the date is squeezed at the stem end, the flesh should pop out of the skin, then you can use a sharp knife to cut the fruit in half and carefully prise out the stone.

The sweet flavour of dates combines very well with vinegar to make a wonderful sweet-and-sour preserve that goes particularly well with cheese. Semi-dried and dried dates are also widely available and can be added to chutneys.

FIGS

These fragile fruits have thin skins that may be purple or greenish gold; inside is a glorious soft, scented flesh filled with tiny round seeds. Fresh figs need careful handling as they damage easily. When figs are ripe and yield to a light pressure, they can be poached whole in syrup for bottling; they do not need to be peeled, simply snip off the tough stem. Avoid sour-smelling figs; this indicates

DRIED FRUITS

All kinds of fruits are available dried and they can successfully be made into jams and pickles, or included in chutneys and relishes. Jams made with dried fruits have a concentrated fruity flavour and often require less sugar than fresh fruit jams. Modern tenderized dried fruit, often labelled "ready-to-eat", requires a short soaking time, or sometimes none at all, before being made into jam. Any soaking liquid may be used as part of the recipe. If the fruit needs to be chopped into small pieces, do this after soaking, or it will absorb too much water.

Many dried fruits, including mangoes, apricots, prunes, figs and pears, make good pickles. Less sugar is needed than with fresh fruit and pre-soaking is unnecessary; the fruit is put straight into sterilized bottles and hot vinegar poured over.

Dried fruits are also good added to chutneys, particularly when vegetables with a high water content such as marrows (large zucchini) and squashes are used. The dried fruits help to soak up the liquid. Chopped or whole small dried fruits may be added part way through cooking. They add flavour and also speed up the time it takes the chutney to thicken. The shorter cooking time helps to retain the fresh flavour of the other ingredients.

Raisins, sultanas (golden raisins) and currants are often referred to as vine fruits and are popularly added to chutneys to give a sweet-and-sour result. They are made from grapes that have been dried in the sun. Raisins are made from seeded and seedless grapes, sultanas are produced from seedless white grapes, and currants from small black grapes.

they are over-ripe. When figs are plentiful, they can be made into luxurious conserves and chutneys. Warm spices such as cinnamon and vanilla go very well with figs. Dried figs, with their concentrated flavour, make a thick, dark

and delicious jam. A little grated orange rind added to the mixture heightens the flavour.

Below: Figs have a subtle, sweet flavour and are particularly good bottled whole in syrup.

VEGETABLE FRUITS

Sweet (bell) peppers, tomatoes and aubergines (eggplant) are fruits, but they are treated like vegetables.

THE PEPPER FAMILY

From mild peppers to hot chillies, this family of vegetable fruits can be preserved in pickles, chutneys or relishes, or used to add flavour and texture to preserves made with a variety of other vegetables.

sweet peppers

These are the mildest members of the capsicum family. Young peppers have a sharp flavour and are bright green. As they mature, they become sweeter and turn yellow, then orange and finally red. Preserved green peppers tend to lose their colour with long-term

Above: Sweet peppers can be used in all savoury preserves. Roasting them first brings out their flavour.

storage, which is unimportant in dark chutneys, but best avoided in clear pickles.

chillies

These small peppers with a spicy kick are the world's most popular spice. Green chillies are immature, while red ones are ripe. As a very general rule, chillies sweeten as they ripen so dark green chillies tend to be hotter than paler green ones and red ones. Heat is influenced by a combination of variety and the climate. Anaheim and Dutch chillies are mild, Jalapeño and Scotch bonnets are much hotter, and tiny Thai or bird's eye chillies are very hot. Dried chillies are used in most pickling spices.

Left: Crisp green peppers are good in dark-coloured relishes.

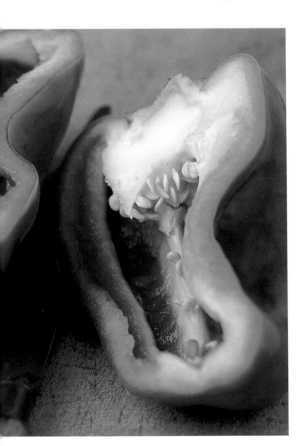

PREPARING FRESH CHILLIES

When handling fresh chillies, either wear gloves or wash your hands in soapy water directly afterwards. Chillies contain capsaicin, which can cause severe irritation to skin, especially on the face.

1 Using a sharp knife, halve the chilli, then cut off and discard the stalk and the very top part of the chilli.

2 Carefully scrape out and discard the seeds and core, then cut out and discard the white membrane, keeping the knife close to the flesh.

3 To chop finely, cut the chilli flesh lengthways into very thin strips, then cut the strips across to make tiny pieces.

TOMATOES

From unripe green tomatoes to ripe red ones, tomatoes are used in all types of pickles and preserves. Ripe tomatoes may be yellow or red, depending on variety and their sweetness or acidity varies according to types as well as how ripe they were when picked. The common round tomato is juicy and fairly acidic. Italian plum tomatoes have an elongated shape with denser flesh and a sweeter flavour. Tiny cherry tomatoes are very sweet, while beefsteak tomatoes are very large and can weigh up to 450g/1lb. Unripe green tomatoes are usually picked at the end of the season when there is not

Above: Tomatoes have tough skins so are often better peeled before adding to pickles and preserves.

enough summer sunshine to ripen them. They are often made into green tomato chutney, but may also be included in tart relishes such as piccalilli. Green tomatoes are slightly bland so are best combined with apples or other fruit and plenty of flavourings.

Ripe tomatoes may be made into sweet jams and marmalades as well as savoury jellies, chutneys, relishes, sauces and pickles. If the tomatoes are not going to be strained after cooking, their tough skins should be removed before cooking; the easiest way to do this is to blanch them first. Ripe tomatoes can also be dried in the oven, then bottled in oil.

Choose firm, unblemished tomatoes, preferably with the calyx intact. Once ripe, they should be preserved as soon as possible, although they can be stored in the salad drawer of the refrigerator for a few days.

PREPARING TOMATOES

1 To peel tomatoes, make a shallow cross at the base of each one. Place in a bowl and pour over boiling water. Leave for 30 seconds, or until the skin curls away at the cut.

2 Drain the tomatoes, dip in cold water and peel.

3 To remove the seeds, cut the tomatoes into quarters and cut out the seeds with a knife.

AUBERGINES/EGGPLANT

The most common aubergines are large, dark purple and oval but there are also smaller round purple ones and a little oval, ivory-white variety that inspired the American name eggplant. Aubergines may be pickled raw, either sliced or whole, but they are more usually chopped and cooked in pickles. Aubergines are often salted when making chutneys and pickles to extract some of the moisture, which would otherwise dilute the mixture. When buying, look for small to medium-size aubergines with smooth and shiny skins; they will have sweet, tender flesh. Larger specimens with wrinkled skins are too mature and may be tough and slightly bitter. Aubergines can be stored in the refrigerator for up to two weeks before preserving.

Below: Baby aubergines are great pickled whole in brine or vinegar with whole spices.

THE ONION FAMILY

ONIONS

These include strongly flavoured brown-skinned onions, used for everyday cooking, and the larger mild, sweet and juicy Spanish onions, which are also known as yellow onions. White onions with papery skins and red onions are mild and sweet, the latter adding a good colour to preserves. All types of onion can be made into onion chutneys and relishes, sliced and pickled in rings, or dried.

Pickling onions have brown papery skins and are also called button or pearl onions. They are main-crop onions, picked when very small. The milder-tasting and smaller silverskin onions, which are harvested when they have a diameter of no more than 2.5cm/1in, can also be pickled. Soaking them in a wet brine for 24–36 hours draws out some of the moisture and gives them a crunchier texture when pickled. It is important to use a stainless steel knife when preparing onions to prevent the cut surfaces of the onion from darkening.

Above: Red onions have a sweet, mild flavour and can add a lovely colour to preserves.

Above: Shallots have a strong flavour and are very good pickled in malt or cider vinegar.

SHALLOTS

These are a different variety of onion, grown in clusters rather than as single bulbs. They have an elongated shape and papery russet skin. Shallots have a fuller, sweeter flavour than onions and are delicious pickled.

SPRING ONIONS

Also known as green onions or scallions, these are young bulb onions, pulled while the tops are still green and before the bulb has had a chance to swell. Long cooking does not suit spring onions, so they are rarely used in chutneys. They may, however, be added to relishes with short cooking times.

PEELING PICKLING ONIONS

1 Place the onions in a bowl and pour over boiling water to cover. Leave for 1–2 minutes.

2 Drain the onions and rinse under cold water to cool. Using a sharp knife, trim the tops and root end, then slip the skins from the onions.

Below: Spring onions can be pickled whole, or chopped and added to relishes and chutneys.

LEEKS

Long, thin leeks are the mildest members of the onion family. They are included in chutneys to add texture and flavour, or pickled on their own. To clean leeks, slit them lengthways and rinse under cold water to remove any trapped grit.

GARLIC

This is the most pungent member of the onion family. One or two cloves can be used to add a subtle flavour to chutney and relishes. Vinegar can be flavoured with garlic, then used to make preserves; peel the cloves and add 5–6 to each 600ml/1 pint/2½ cups vinegar. Leave for 2 weeks to infuse. Use within 4 months.

Above: Garlic can be pickled whole, or used as a flavouring in all kinds of savoury preserves.

MUSHROOMS

There are dozens of edible mushrooms. The common cultivated mushroom is sold at various stages in its growth. Button (white) mushrooms are the youngest and these are the best for pickling and preserving as they are firm and their round, compact shape means that they are less likely to be damaged by packing into jars. When the cap has partially opened, mushrooms are sold as cup mushrooms and, when opened out completely, as flat or Portabello mushrooms. The larger they grow, the more flavour they have and the darker their juices. Mushroom varieties such as pale,

fan-shaped oyster and dark brown, cup-shaped shiitake are less suitable for preserves because they lose their delicate texture and become rubbery. Buy really fresh firm-textured mushrooms and preserve promptly after buying. Wipe them clean with a damp cloth and wash only if very dirty; do not leave mushrooms to soak. Keep them whole or halve or quarter them, depending on size. Mushrooms are often flavoured with herbs such as dill, and warm spices such as mace. They can also be dried successfully – shiitake mushrooms and wild fungi dry particularly well.

Above: Large flat mushrooms have a good, strong flavour and a rich, dark colour so are perfect for making into mushroom ketchup.

ROOTS AND TUBERS

Vegetables that grow underground include roots such as carrots and turnips, and tubers such as potatoes and Jerusalem artichokes. Roots and tubers tend to become starchier with age, so they are usually preserved while young, sweet and tender.

Above: Baby carrots are delicious pickled whole in spiced vinegar.

BEETROOT/BEET

Dark ruby-red beetroot has a rich, earthy, sweet flavour and is one of the most commonly preserved root vegetables. Pickled beetroot is eaten throughout Europe, and sweet-and-sour Harvard beets are popular in the United States. There are two varieties of beetroot: globe and a long, slender variety. The former is usually preserved whole and the latter sliced into rounds.

When preparing beetroot, be careful not to damage the skin, or the colour will leach out. Trim the stalks to 2.5cm/1in above the root. When pickling whole, choose even-size beetroot that require the same cooking time; small beetroot are preferable as they are sweeter and more tender than larger ones.

CARROTS

These sweet-tasting orange roots can be chopped or grated and used in chutneys, relishes and wonderful sweet jams. Carrot jam probably originated during the Second World War, when fruit was scarce, but it is every bit as good as fruit jams and can be made more luxurious with the addition of almonds and citrus flavouring.

PARSNIPS, SWEDES/RUTABAGAS AND TURNIPS

Closely related to the carrot, but with a sweeter taste and a nutty flavour, creamy-coloured parsnips should be scrubbed before preserving and peeled if tough. Use young vegetables because large roots can be very woody.

The globe-shaped swede has creamy orange flesh and a delicate, sweet flavour.

Right: Tender, crunchy baby turnips are excellent pickled.

Above: Big, knobbly celeriac have a distinctive yet delicate flavour.

Turnips are smaller than swede, and they have a smoother skin and white flesh with a peppery flavour. Tender young spring turnips are ideal for pickling and preserving.

CELERIAC

Related to celery, this knobbly root has a similar flavour. In shape and size it looks a bit like a rough-skinned swede (rutabaga), but the flesh is ivory coloured. It should be thickly peeled before using and immediately immersed in acidulated water to prevent it from turning brown. Choose small celeriac, as older ones can be stringy and may have large hollows in the flesh. Celeriac can be cubed and added to chutneys instead of celery or coarsely shredded and pickled with other root vegetables such as carrots. Dill and orange go especially well with celeriac.

RADISHES

These have a refreshing, but very peppery flavour. The familiar small round or slightly elongated red or white varieties are sold all year round. The white Japanese radish, known as mooli or daikon, is considerably larger and longer; it looks like a large, very smooth parsnip. Mooli has a mild flavour and can be cut into paper-thin slices and pickled.

HORSERADISH

This extremely pungent root is never eaten as a vegetable. The knobbly root is peeled and then grated before being made into a condiment, usually with oil and vinegar. The astringency of its flavour makes horseradish the perfect accompaniment for rich or fatty foods. The vapours that are given off while grating horseradish are extremely irritating and quite unpleasant but the end result makes the process worthwhile.

KOHLRABI

The edible part of kohlrabi is the stalk or tuber that swells above the ground. They are similar to turnips in size, appearance and taste. It is best to use small kohlrabi, no more than 5cm/2in across, for preserving because they toughen with age and their flesh becomes course and fibrous. To prepare kohlrabi, trim off the base and leaves, and peel thinly. Put the cut vegetable into acidulated water immediately to prevent it browning. Use sliced or chopped in chutneys.

Below: Tiny, peppery radishes are delicious pickled and served with cold meats or cheeses.

JERUSALEM ARTICHOKES

These small, knobbly tubers have a delicious nutty, sweet flavour when cooked. Peeling off the brown skin is time-consuming but essential – use a swivel-bladed peeler or a small sharp paring knife. These tasty vegetables can be used in chutneys and are delicious in spicy Indian relishes.

PREVENTING DISCOLORATION

Many vegetables, including parsnips, radishes, celeriac and Jerusalem artichokes, discolour very quickly when their cut flesh is exposed to air. To avoid discoloration, always prepare these vegetables with a stainless steel rather than a carbon-steel knife, and prevent the flesh browning either by submerging them or blanching them in acidulated water.

Acidulated water In a large bowl, combine 30ml/2 tbsp vinegar or lemon juice for every 600ml/1 pint/2½ cups cold water. Add the vegetables and keep them immersed by weighing them down with a plate. Use as soon as possible.

Blanching Make a paste with 15ml/1 tbsp plain (all-purpose) flour and 45ml/3 tbsp cold water, then stir in 30ml/ 2 tbsp lemon juice. Whisk the paste into a pan of salted boiling water, then add the vegetables and blanch them briefly before preserving.

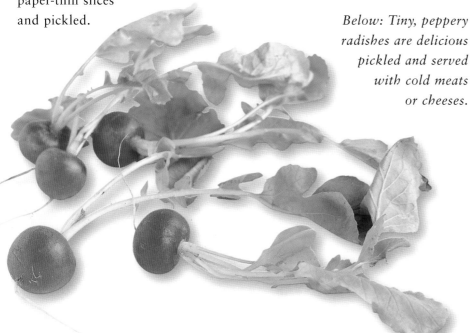

SQUASHES

There are two main categories of this vegetable: summer squash and winter squash, but most are now available all year round. They vary in size and shape from small, dark green courgettes (zucchini) to large, round, orange pumpkins.

Above: Butternut squash has sweet orange flesh that is great added to chutneys and pickles.

WINTER SQUASHES

These squashes have tough inedible skins, fibrous flesh and large seeds, and include butternut squash, acorn squash, and pumpkins. Their dense, sweet flesh cooks to a thick pulp and can be made into tasty jams but they can also be used to add sweetness and a rich orange colour to chutneys.

SUMMER SQUASHES

When young and immature, these squashes have thin, edible skins and seeds. They are used to make chutneys, but may also be made into relishes and salsas because they become tender after a fairly short cooking time.

marrows

Known as large zucchini in the United States, marrows have a pleasant, but bland, flavour and high water content, so they are best brined before making into chutney. Although the skin is edible, it is quite tough so marrows are usually peeled, and the seeds discarded. Marrow can be combined with stronger tasting vegetables and warm spices such as ginger.

Right: Courgettes are best pickled when young and tender.

Above: Mild tasting cucumbers are perfect for pickles and relishes.

cucumbers

Due to their high water content, cucumbers are usually brined before preserving. As a rule, small ridged cucumbers are pickled; long salad ones are used in relishes.

courgettes/zucchini

Picked when small, courgettes have a dark green shiny skin with light streaks, and creamy coloured flesh. The seeds are very tender.

patty pan squashes

Shaped like flying saucers, patty pan squashes are green, yellow or striped. They look attractive cut into triangular wedges, then pickled.

BRASSICAS

This family of vegetables range from pale leafy Chinese leaves (Chinese cabbage) to compact Brussels sprouts. Cabbages and cauliflower, in particular, are widely used in pickles, chutneys and relishes. Softer leafy greens such as spinach, spring greens (collards) and Swiss chard, are less suited to preserving because they discolour and lose their texture.

CABBAGES

The many types of cabbage range from dark green, crinkly-leafed Savoy to smooth, tightly wrapped white cabbages. From a preserving point of view, it is the firm white and red cabbages that are most suitable. Red cabbage is similar to white cabbage in texture, but has a sweeter taste and takes slightly longer to cook. If it needs to be blanched before preserving, a little vinegar should be added to the

Below: Firm red cabbage can be made into a delicious pickle with a fabulous dark pink hue.

water to help retain the red colour. Preserved cabbage is found in many cuisines, from the German fermented sauerkraut to sour Korean *kimchee*, which is flavoured with ginger, chilli and garlic. Hot and warm spices such as caraway seeds and juniper berries, go particularly well with cabbage. Choose firm, young cabbages and discard any tough outer leaves.

CAULIFLOWER

The creamy white florets of this mild-flavoured brassica feature in many savoury preserves, notably piccalilli, in which it is lightly cooked to retain its shape and crisp texture. It soaks up spices well and so is often used in hot and spicy Indian pickles and chutneys. When buying, check that the florets are not discoloured and that the remaining leaves are fresh and green, not yellow and wilted.

Above: Firm, white cauliflower is delicious broken into florets and pickled.

BROCCOLI

Dark green broccoli isn't often used in preserves because it tends to discolour when stored for any length of time. The long cooking required for chutneys would make the broccoli disintegrate, so cut it into tiny florets and add towards the end of the cooking time in piccalilli and relishes.

MAKING SAUERKRAUT
This classic pickled cabbage from Germany has a sharp, pungent flavour that goes very well with meats and cheeses.

1 Finely shred 1.2kg/2½lb white cabbage. Toss it with 25g/1oz coarse kosher salt and 7.5ml/ 1½ tsp spices such as caraway seeds, crushed juniper berries and black peppercorns. Leave the cabbage to stand for about 10 minutes, mix again, then pack into a large sterilized crock or bowl, pressing down well.

2 Weight the cabbage with a large plate, cover the crock or bowl with a lid and leave it in a cool place (below 20°C/70°F) for 1 week.

3 Remove the plate and skim off any scum with a spoon. Repeat daily for about 1 month until no more scum appears. (This means that the cabbage has stopped fermenting and it is ready.)

4 Pack into sterilized jars, cover and store in the refrigerator for up to 1 month.

SHOOTS

These tender vegetables have mild but distinctive flavours and are very good used in preserves.

ASPARAGUS

White and purple asparagus are grown in Spain, Holland and France under mounds of earth and picked just as the tips begin to show, while the spears of green asparagus, popular in Britain and America, develop their colour because it grows above ground. Asparagus can be included in luxurious preserves. Use when very fresh; the stalks should be firm and the tips plump.

Below: Young tender asparagus makes a very upmarket chutney to serve with light meats or shellfish.

FENNEL

Florence fennel has squat, plump bulbs with a similar texture to celery, and green feathery fronds. It has a mild aniseed flavour that mellows and sweetens when pickled. Keep it in the refrigerator and use within a few days, while the bulb is firm and the greenery still fresh. Use white wine or sherry vinegar without pickling spices. Small fennel bulbs can be pickled whole; larger ones should be halved or quartered. Blanch the fennel in brine, then leave to cool; pack into jars and top up with cold vinegar. Chopped fennel can be added to chutneys, and the green fronds may be chopped and used in apple jelly.

CELERY

Crisp, crunchy celery may have white or green stalks, which should snap easily and not bend. Celery does not make a good pickle on its own, but is often added to mixed pickles, chutneys and relishes. Wrapped in a plastic bag, celery will keep in the refrigerator for a week or more. Sometimes the outside stalks are removed and the top of the celery trimmed, leaving the sweet celery hearts.

GLOBE ARTICHOKES

These look like enormous thistle-heads with purple-tinged green leaves. They are difficult to preserve whole, but the hearts can be pickled in a mild vinegar, such as white wine or cider (apple cider) vinegar, then drizzled with olive oil to serve.

Above: Globe artichokes are difficult to preserve whole, but their leaves can be removed and the hearts preserved in vinegar.

PREPARING GLOBE ARTICHOKES

1 Hold the artichoke firmly and, using a sharp knife, cut off the stalk close to the base.

2 Peel away the leaves from the artichoke, rubbing the exposed parts with lemon juice to stop them browning.

3 Trim the artichoke heart with a paring knife, removing any tough areas and rubbing frequently with lemon juice.

4 Using a teaspoon, scoop out and discard the hairy choke from the middle of the artichoke, then immerse the heart in a bowl of cold water with 30ml/2 tbsp lemon juice.

PODS AND SEEDS

This group of vegetables, which includes peas, beans and corn, are all good in chutneys and relishes.

PEAS

Fresh peas in their pods have a delicate sweet flavour and make a tasty addition to chutneys and relishes. They should be added about 10 minutes before the end of cooking time, so that they stay firm and keep their colour.

BROAD/FAVA BEANS

These can be used in the same way as peas, but choose young fresh ones because the skins become tough as the beans mature.

GREEN BEANS

All types of green beans can be used to add flavour, colour and texture to preserves. French beans are small, narrow green beans with round pods that are available all year round;

Above: Corn kernels can be stripped from the cobs and used to make a delicious relish.

American green beans are similar, but much larger; flat runner beans are popular in Britain and are at their best when the home-grown crop is available in summer. Top and tail beans before use; some varieties of runner beans, and particularly older ones, may need stringing.

Below: Broad beans, runner beans and French beans can all be added to chutneys and preserves.

SWEETCORN

Corn cobs should be used as soon as possible after picking, before their natural sugars turn to starch. Choose cobs with plump, fresh kernels that are unwrinkled and show no signs of browning. Shuck the cobs and strip off the kernels using a sharp knife. Baby corn cobs have a more delicate flavour than mature ones; they can be sliced into rounds and used in the same ways. Store corn cobs in the refrigerator for no more than a few days.

DRIED BEANS
These can be pickled or added to chutneys and relishes. The beans need to be soaked, then boiled for 10 minutes before simmering in unsalted boiling water until tender. They can then be drained and bottled in vinegar flavoured with fresh herbs or spices. Cooked beans can also be added to chutneys and relishes – stir them in about 10 minutes before the end of the cooking time.

HERBS AND FLOWERS

Flavourings are an essential part of most preserves and using the right amount is as important as selecting the correct one. In some preserves a subtle hint is all that is needed; in others the flavouring is one of the main ingredients.

HERBS

Fresh and dried herbs are invaluable in savoury preserves, and are included occasionally in sweet ones. They can be added during the initial cooking, then removed, or finely chopped and stirred in towards the end of cooking. If dried herbs are used instead of fresh, then reduce the quantity by a third to half.

Below: Oregano has a lovely, aromatic flavour that is very good with summer squashes.

tender herbs

Herbs with fragile leaves need careful handling to avoid bruising. Once picked, they should be used within a few days. Tie the whole herb stalks in muslin (cheesecloth) and add to the simmering preserve, or stir chopped leaves into the preserve at the end of cooking.

Basil This highly aromatic herb bruises and discolours easily, so rather than adding it to a preserve, it can be steeped in vinegar until it imparts its flavour, then removed.

Chervil Use these tiny, soft and lacy leaves soon after picking. They have a flavour similar to parsley with a hint of aniseed, which goes well with mild, delicate vegetables.

Mint The many varieties of this aromatic herb include peppermint, spearmint, apple mint, lemon mint and pineapple mint. It adds a fresh flavour to preserves, but should be used sparingly.

Parsley Curly and flat leaf varieties are available. It is an essential herb in a bouquet garni.

Tarragon This herb is excellent for flavouring vinegars but is rarely used in its fresh form because it darkens and discolours on heating.

robust herbs

Often woody, with pungent leaves, these herbs are added to preserves during cooking to extract and mellow their flavour.

Bay leaf Essential in bouquet garni, these dark green glossy leaves should be dried for a few days before use. They add a slightly spicy flavour to preserves.

Above: Parsley has a mild flavour and is often used with other herbs.

Marjoram and oregano Popular in tomato preserves, these herbs are also good with marrow (large zucchini). They should be added towards the end of cooking.

Rosemary Powerfully aromatic, fresh or dried rosemary should be used in small quantities. It goes very well with citrus fruits.

Sage A strong herb that often partners garlic and tomatoes.

Thyme This robust herb works well with preserves made from roasted vegetables and beans.

aromatic and spicy herbs

Some herbs have aromatic citrus flavours, others aniseed tones; a few have a warm, spicy pungency.

Coriander/cilantro Every part of this aromatic herb can be used – from its delicate leaves and sturdier stalks to its hard brown seeds. Also known as Chinese parsley, the leaves resemble slightly rounded flat leaf parsley. They have an warm, spicy taste and add pungency to Middle Eastern, Asian and Indian chutneys and fresh, Mexican-style relishes.

Dill This delicate herb has dark green, feathery leaves and has a subtle aniseed taste. It is an excellent flavouring for mild-tasting courgette (zucchini) and cucumber relishes and pickles.

Fennel Part of the same family as dill, with a similar, but stronger flavour, it is particularly good for flavouring vinegars.

Kaffir lime leaf This strong-tasting, aromatic leaf is used to flavour Thai and Malaysian preserves.

Lemon grass A tall hard grass, with a distinctive lemony aroma and taste, lemon grass is often used in Thai preserves and should be bruised to release the flavour.

Lovage Similar to celery leaves with a peppery flavour, lovage is good with root vegetables and in mixed vegetable chutneys.

FLOWERS

Many types of edible flowers and their leaves can be used to add fragrance and flavour to preserves, including the flowers of herbs such as rosemary, thyme, marjoram, fennel and chives.

Borage The tiny, brilliant blue or purple flowers of this plant can be candied or used to decorate jellies. Borage leaves have a fresh cucumber-like taste and can be used to flavour jellies.

Geranium leaves These give jams and jellies a subtle flavour. There are several different varieties with apple, rose or lemon aromas.

Lavender Intensely fragrant, sprigs of lavender can be used to flavour sugar, jams and jellies. The sprigs also look very pretty suspended in jelly: dip them in boiling water first, then shake off the excess before putting them in the jar and pouring over the hot jelly.

Rose Scented red, pink or yellow petals make wonderful jams and jellies. They are often combined with fruit juice, such as grape, and with added pectin, so that the preserve sets quickly without destroying the aroma of the petals. Be sure to use unsprayed roses.

Left: Tender-leafed basil has a fragrant, peppery flavour that goes particularly well with tomato-based preserves.

MAKING A BOUQUET GARNI

This is a bunch of aromatic herbs, tied with a piece of string or in a square of muslin (cheesecloth). A bouquet garni can be added to preserves and simmered until the flavours have infused into the mixture, giving a subtle taste and aroma. Fresh herbs will give the best flavour.

1 For jellies or sauces that will be strained after cooking, tie together a sprig of parsley, a sprig of thyme, and a bay leaf with a piece of string. Suspend the bunch of herbs in the preserve, tying it to the pan handle for easy removal.

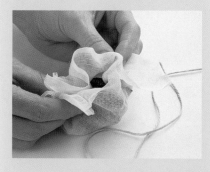

2 For chutneys and relishes, tie the herbs loosely in a piece of fine muslin (cheesecloth), about 15cm/6in square, so that the liquid can bubble through and extract the herbs' flavour.

SPICES

These can be hot and spicy or warm and fragrant and are used in all kinds of preserves both for flavour and decoration. Store spices in a cool, dark place: ground ones will keep for up to six months, whole spices for a year.

HOT SPICES

These spices are used to add heat to preserves, and can be mild and subtle or exceedingly fiery.

Cayenne Made from ground dried chillies, cayenne is extremely hot and should be used sparingly.

Chillies Fresh chillies may be cooked in preserves to add heat, or added whole or chopped to clear pickles when bottling.

Below: Sweet, mild paprika is used to add both flavour and colour to chutneys and relishes.

Chilli powder This hot spice is made from ground dried chillies. Mild chilli powder and chilli seasoning are both blends of ground chilli and milder spices such as cumin, oregano and garlic.

Galangal Related to ginger, with pink-tinged flesh, galangal is often used in Malasian- and Thai-style preserves. Ginger may be used as a substitute.

Ginger Good in both sweet and savoury preserves, root ginger may be used fresh, dried or ground. Preserved stem ginger can be added to conserves and marmalades.

Mustard There are three types of mustard seed: white, brown and black; the latter is the hottest. The taste and aroma develops when the seeds are crushed or mixed with liquid. Whole mustard seeds are often included in pickles and ground mustard powder in relishes. The intensity diminishes with long simmering, so mustard powder is often added towards the end of cooking. Salt and vinegar also reduce its pungency.

Paprika This rich, red spice is sold ground and used for its colour and flavour, which ranges from mild and sweet to strong and pungent.

Peppercorns Often added whole to pickles, these tiny round berries may be green, black or white. Green ones are unripe and mildly flavoured, black ones are hot and pungent. White peppercorns have a mild aromatic flavour.

Turmeric Although yellow turmeric has a distinctive warm, spicy taste, it is often used simply for its colour as a cheap alternative to saffron in pickles and relishes.

Above: Fresh root ginger adds warmth and a lively fresh flavour to all kinds of preserves.

SEED SPICES

Some plants such as coriander and dill are cultivated for both their leaves and seeds; others, including caraway and cumin, are grown for their seeds alone.

Caraway seeds These are mildly pungent and feature in many northern European preserves, notably sauerkraut. The seeds need long soaking or cooking to soften them and release the flavour.

Cumin seeds Tiny light brown seeds with a distinctive warm flavour, cumin is used in Indian, Mexican, North African and Middle Eastern preserves. Cumin seeds are widely available both whole and ground.

GRINDING WHOLE SPICES

Spices may be bought ready-ground but most are best when freshly ground because, once ground, they quickly lose their flavour and aroma. Grind spices by hand using a mortar and pestle, or use a spice mill or coffee grinder reserved solely for this purpose.

Above: Whole cinnamon sticks are often used to flavour sweet syrups for preserving fruits.

Coriander seeds These small round seeds have a mild-orange flavour and taste very different from the green leafy herb. They are usually included in pickling spice.

Dill seeds Small oval seeds with a similar flavour to caraway, these are often used with cucumber pickles and relishes.

FRAGRANT SPICES

Spices with a warm, fragrant flavour are good used in both fruity and sweet preserves.

Allspice With an aroma and flavour that is reminiscent of cloves, cinnamon and nutmeg, this is good used with orchard fruits.

Cassia and cinnamon The bark of evergreen trees, these are available ground or in sticks. The sticks are best used whole for flavouring pale or clear preserves.

Cloves These tiny dried flower buds, sold whole or ground, have a distinctive taste that goes well with apples and citrus fruit.

Juniper Used to give gin its distinctive flavour, blue-black juniper berries may be used fresh, but are more usually dried.

Nutmeg and mace Nutmeg has a warm nutty flavour. It is best bought whole and grated fresh. Mace is the orange-coloured lacy outer covering of the nutmeg; it is sold as blades.

Saffron Made from the dried stigmas of the *Crocus sativus*, saffron is the most expensive of all spices. Only a few threads are needed to produce a golden colour and impart a bitter-sweet flavour.

Star anise This star-shaped, aniseed-flavoured spice looks wonderful in pickles and bottled preserves. It can also be used sparingly in chutneys.

Tamarind This dark brown pulp from the pod of the tamarind tree adds a unique sour flavour to preserves and pickles.

Left: Golden saffron threads can be used to impart a subtle flavour and glorious colour.

Vanilla Used to flavour bottled fruits and occasionally jams and jellies, long, dark brown vanilla pods (beans) have a sweet, warm, aromatic flavour. The pods can be re-used if rinsed thoroughly, dried and stored in an airtight jar.

PICKLING SPICES

Various blends of pickling spices are available. It is worth searching for a preferred blend or making your own. Typical mixtures include allspice, bay leaf, cardamom, coriander and mustard seeds, cassia or cinnamon, dried chillies, whole cloves, dried root ginger and peppercorns. Add 5–15ml/1–3 tsp of pickling spices to each 600ml/ 1 pint/2½ cups vinegar and simmer for 5–15 minutes, then cool and strain. Alternatively, tie the spices in muslin (cheesecloth), cook them in the preserve, then remove.

Below: Vanilla, star anise, ground ginger and cinnamon sticks are all widely used in preserves.

PRESERVING INGREDIENTS

A few special ingredients are essential when making preserves, because they contribute to the keeping quality of the final jam, jelly or pickle. The four main preservatives are sugar, vinegar, salt and alcohol. These all help to prolong the life of the other ingredients used in the preserve by creating an environment in which micro-organisms such as moulds and bacteria cannot grow.

SUGAR

This is the key preservative used in jams, jellies, marmalades, curds and many preserved fruits. A high proportion of sugar is needed and if the sugar content is less than 60 per cent of the total weight of the preserve (for example, in low-sugar jams), this will affect the keeping quality of the preserve. These low-sugar jams and fruit preserves should be used within a few months or kept in the refrigerator to prevent the growth of mould.

Sugar also plays an important role in the setting of jams, jellies and marmalades. To achieve a good set, sugar should make up between 55 and 70 per cent of the total weight of the preserve. (High acid content in the fruit makes the exact amount of sugar less crucial.)

white sugars

These refined sugars produce clear, set, sweet preserves.
Preserving sugar has quite large, irregular crystals and is ideal for jams, jellies and marmalades. The large crystals allow water to percolate between them, which helps to prevent the preserve burning and reduces the need for stirring (which is important to avoid breaking up fruit too much). Use this sugar for the clearest preserves. If preserving sugar is unavailable, granulated sugar can be used instead.
Preserving sugar with pectin Also known as jam sugar, this sugar is used with low-pectin fruit. The sugar contains natural pectin and citric acid to help overcome setting problems. Preserves made with this sugar tend to have a shorter shelf-life and should be stored for no longer than six months.

Left: White and golden sugars are a key ingredient used in sweet fruit preserves, jams and jellies.

Granulated sugar is slightly coarser than caster (superfine) sugar, less expensive and gives a clear result.
Cube sugar is made from white granulated sugar that has been moistened, moulded into blocks, dried and cubed. It gives the same results as preserving sugar.

brown sugars

These sugars give a pronounced flavour and darker colour to both sweet and savoury preserves.
Demerara/raw sugar is a pale golden sugar with a mild caramel flavour. Traditionally an unrefined sugar with a low molasses content, it may also be made from refined white sugar with molasses added.
Golden granulated sugar may be refined or unrefined. It can be used instead of white sugar for a hint of flavour and colour.
Soft brown sugar is moist, with fine grains and a rich flavour. It may be light or dark in colour and is usually made from refined white sugar with molasses added.
Muscovado/molasses sugar may be light or dark and is usually made from unrefined cane sugar. It has a deeper, more pronounced taste than soft brown sugar.
Palm sugar is made from the sap of palms and has a fragrant flavour. Sold pressed into blocks, it needs to be chopped before use. Light muscovado (brown) sugar is a good alternative.
Jaggery is a raw sugar from India with a distinctive taste. It must be chopped before use. Use a mixture of light brown muscovado and demerara sugar as an alternative.

Right: Raspberry and white wine vinegar are used both to preserve ingredients and to add a sharp, tangy flavour.

VINEGARS

The word vinegar comes from the French *vin aigre*, meaning sour wine. Vinegar is made by exposing fruit or grain-based alcohol to air; a bacterial reaction then turns the alcohol into acetic acid and it is this acid that helps to prevent the growth of micro-organisms in pickles and preserves. Vinegar used for pickling must have an acetic acid content of at least 5 per cent.

Malt vinegar is made from a type of beer. It usually has an acetic acid content of 8 per cent, which allows it to be safely diluted by moisture and juices from fruit and vegetables. Malt vinegar usually contains caramel, which turns it a dark brown colour. Its strong flavour makes it ideal for pickles, chutneys and bottled sauces.

Pickling vinegar is simply malt vinegar flavoured with spices.

Distilled malt vinegar has the same strong flavour as ordinary malt vinegar but is colourless and therefore suitable for making clear pickles and light preserves.

Wine vinegar may be red or white, depending on the colour of the original wine. Most wine vinegars contain about 6 per cent acetic acid. White wine vinegar is mild and better for delicate preserves; red wine vinegar is slightly more robust and good for spiced fruits.

Raspberry vinegar, made by steeping the fruit in wine vinegar, is excellent for pickled fruits.

Balsamic vinegar has a smooth, mellow flavour. Its low acidity makes it unsuitable for use on its own, but it can be used as a flavouring for mild preserves, stirred in at the end of cooking.

Sherry vinegar is slightly sweet with a fairly strong flavour.

Cider vinegar has a slightly sharp taste and a fruity flavour. It is excellent for fruit preserves.

Rice vinegar Colourless, mild rice vinegar is made from rice wine and is often used for pickling ginger.

SALT

This is used in preserving both as a seasoning and as a dehydrator. It is often used in a process called brining to draw out moisture from vegetables such as cucumber and marrow, making them crisp and preventing the dilution of the preserve, which would reduce its keeping quality. Ordinary table and cooking salt is fine for this process, but use pure crystal salt, also known as kosher salt, or preserving or rock salt for clear pickles as ordinary table and cooking salts contain anti-caking ingredients that cause clouding.

ALCOHOL

Spirits, such as brandy and rum, and liqueurs, which are at least 40% ABV (alcohol by volume), can be used. Fortified wine, wine, beer and cider have a lower alcohol content so are not effective alone and should be either heat treated or combined with sugar.

ACIDS

These help to set jams and jellies and prevent discoloration.

Lemon juice adds pectin, prevents fruits from turning brown and enhances both flavour and colour. Use either freshly squeezed or bottled lemon juice.

Citric acid is sold as fine white crystals and can be used instead of lemon juice in preserves.

Tamarind is a spice used both for its acid flavour and its character.

Above: Many different kinds of salt – from coarse sea salt to preserving salt can be used for pickling.

preserving techniques

From jewel-like jams and jellies to sweet fruits preserved in sugar syrups and alcohol, and from spicy chutneys and relishes to tart sauces and pickles, there are so many fabulous ways to preserve fresh fruits and vegetables that it's sometimes hard to know where to begin. This easy-to-follow guide leads you through all the main preserving techniques, offering advice on how to preserve and how to avoid the potential pitfalls.

POTTING AND COVERING PRESERVES

Make sure you have enough jars and bottles, and the correct sterilizing equipment before you start to make any preserve. Preparing, covering and storing preserves correctly helps to ensure the preserve retains its colour, flavour and texture.

CHOOSING CONTAINERS

To make the most of preserves, always pot them in the right type of container. Pickles made from whole or large pieces of fruit or vegetables should be packed into medium or large jars or bottles with a wide neck. Smooth, pourable sauces or relishes can be stored in narrow-necked bottles, but thicker, spoonable preserves should be packed in jars. It is generally better to pack preserves into several smaller containers rather than one large one, especially those that need to be consumed soon after opening.

STERILIZING JARS AND BOTTLES

Before potting, it is essential to sterilize jars and bottles to destroy any micro-organisms in containers. An unsterilized jar or bottle may contain contamination that could cause the preserve to deteriorate or become inedible. Sterilizing is important for all containers, but you should take particular care when re-using jars and bottles.

Check jars and bottles for cracks or damage, then wash thoroughly in hot, soapy water, rinse well and turn upside-down to drain. Jars and bottles may be sterilized in five different ways: by heating in a low oven, immersing in boiling water, heating in a microwave, hot-washing in a dishwasher, or using sterilizing tablets.

Below: Medium, wide-necked jars with plastic-coated screw-top lids are ideal for most preserves.

oven method

Stand the containers, spaced slightly apart, on a baking sheet lined with kitchen paper. Rest any lids on top. Place in a cold oven, then heat to 110°C/225°F/Gas ¼ and bake for 30 minutes. Leave to cool slightly before filling. (If the jars or bottles are not used immediately, cover with a clean cloth and warm again before use.)

boiling water method

1 Place the containers, open-end up, in a deep pan that is wide enough to hold them in one layer.

2 Pour enough hot water into the pan to cover the containers. (Do not use boiling water because this can crack glass.) Bring the water to the boil and boil for 10 minutes.

3 Leave the containers in the pan until the water stops bubbling, then carefully remove and drain upside-down on a clean dishtowel. Turn the containers upright and leave to air-dry for a few minutes.

4 Immerse lids, seals and corks in simmering water for 20 seconds. (Only ever use corks once.)

MAKING CONSERVES

These are very similar to jams, but they have a slightly softer set and contain whole, or large pieces of fruit. The fruit is first mixed with sugar and sometimes a little liquid, then allowed to stand for several hours or even days. The sugar draws out the juices from the fruit, making it firmer and minimizing the cooking time needed. The fruit should be just ripe and even in size. Not all fruit is suitable for making conserves; tough fruit skins do not soften when sugar is added, so fruit such as gooseberries are no good for making conserves.

making strawberry conserve

This preserve takes several days to make, so be sure to leave plenty of time for preparation.

Makes about 1.3kg/3lb

INGREDIENTS

1.3kg/3lb small or medium strawberries, hulled

1.3kg/3lb/generous 6¾ cups granulated sugar

1 Layer the hulled strawberries in a large bowl with the sugar. Cover with clear film (plastic wrap) and chill for 24 hours.

2 Transfer the strawberries, sugar and juices to a large heavy pan. Heat gently, stirring occasionally, until the sugar has dissolved. Bring to the boil and cook steadily (not rapidly) for 5 minutes.

3 Leave the mixture to cool, then place in a bowl, cover with clear film and chill for 2 days.

4 Pour the strawberry mixture into a large pan, bring to the boil and cook steadily for 10 minutes, then remove from the heat and set aside for 10 minutes. Stir, then ladle into warmed sterilized jars and seal.

flavouring conserves

Conserves are more luxurious than jams and often include dried fruit, nuts and spirits or liqueurs. These extra ingredients should be added after setting point is reached.

When adding dried fruit or nuts, chop them evenly and allow about 50g/2oz/½ cup fruit or nuts per 750g/1⅔lb conserve.

Choose spirits or liqueurs that complement the flavour of the chosen fruit. For example, add apricot brandy or amaretto liqueur to apricot conserve, kirsch to cherry conserve and ginger wine to melon conserve; allow 30ml/2 tbsp to every 750g/1⅔lb conserve.

TOP TIPS FOR SUCCESSFUL JAM-MAKING

- Always use the freshest fruit possible and avoid overripe fruit.

- If you wash the fruit, dry it well and use promptly because it will deteriorate on standing.

- Cook the fruit very slowly at first over a low heat to extract the maximum amount of juice and pectin. Stir the fruit frequently until very tender, but do not overcook. (Fruit skins toughen once sugar is added.)

- Warm the sugar in a low oven for about 10 minutes before adding it to the fruit. This will help it to dissolve.

- Stir the preserve to ensure the sugar is completely dissolved before boiling.

- Do not stir frequently when boiling. This lowers the temperature and delays reaching setting point.

- It is wasteful to remove scum too often. To help prevent scum from forming, add a small amount of unsalted (sweet) butter (about 15g/½oz/1 tbsp for every 450g/1lb fruit) when you add the sugar.

- Do not move freshly potted preserves until they are cool and have set completely.

MAKING JELLIES

Jellies are made using the juice strained from simmered fruit, which is then boiled with sugar to setting point. There is very little preparation of fruit, other than giving it a quick rinse and roughly chopping larger fruit, but you do need to allow plenty of time to make the jelly itself. The secret to a beautifully clear jelly lies in straining the fruit pulp through a jelly bag, drip by drip, which takes several hours.

The basic principles of jelly-making are the same as those for jam and the same three substances – pectin, sugar and acid – are needed for the jelly to set. A perfectly set jelly should retain its shape and quiver when spooned out of the jar. Fruits that are low in pectin such as strawberries, cherries and pears are not suitable on their own for making jellies, so are usually combined with high-pectin fruit.

Because the fruit pulp is discarded in jelly-making, the yield is not as large as in jam-making. For this reason many jelly recipes have evolved to make the most of wild fruits, which are free, or gluts of home-grown fruit.

Jellies can be served both as sweet and savoury preserves. Some, such as redcurrant, rowan and cranberry jellies, are classic accompaniments for hot or cold roasted meat or game, or are added to gravy for flavour and give an attractive glossy finish. Savoury jellies often contain chopped herbs and sometimes wine vinegar or cider vinegar to give it a sharper flavour. Sweet jellies may be eaten as a spread.

yield of jelly

The final yield of jelly depends on how juicy the fruit is, and this can vary depending on the time of the year, the weather during growth and its ripeness when harvested. Because of this, the juice, rather than the fruit, is measured and the amount of sugar is calculated accordingly. As a general rule, 450g/1lb/2¼ cups sugar is added for each 600ml/1 pint/2½ cups juice. (If the fruit is very rich in pectin, the recipe may suggest adding slightly less sugar.) As a rough guide, recipes containing 450g/1lb/2¼ cups sugar will make about 675–800g/1½–1¾lb jelly.

making redcurrant jelly

Makes about 1.3kg/3lb

INGREDIENTS

1.3kg/3lb just-ripe redcurrants
600ml/1 pint/2½ cups water
about 900g/2lb/4½ cups preserving or granulated sugar

1 Check the fruit is clean. If necessary, rinse in cold water and use a little less water in the recipe.

2 Remove the currants from the stalks. There is no need to top and tail the fruit.

3 Place the redcurrants in a large heavy pan with the water and simmer gently for about 30 minutes, or until the fruit is very soft and pulpy. Stir occasionally during cooking to prevent the fruit from catching and burning.

4 Pour the cooked fruit and juices into a sterilized jelly bag suspended over a large bowl. Leave to drain for about 4 hours, or until the juice stops dripping. (Do not press or squeeze the fruit in the bag because this will result in a cloudy jelly.)

5 Discard the pulp remaining in the bag (unless you plan to boil the pulp a second time – see page 54). Pour the juice into the cleaned pan and add 450g/1lb/2¼ cups warmed sugar for each 600ml/1 pint/2½ cups of juice. (When making jellies with low-pectin fruit or vegetables, stir in a little lemon juice or vinegar to improve the set. This will also help to offset the sweetness of the jelly.)

6 Heat the mixture gently, stirring frequently, until the sugar has completely dissolved, then increase the heat and bring to the boil.

7 Boil the jelly rapidly for about 10 minutes, or until setting point is reached. You can check this using the flake test or wrinkle test, or you can use a jam thermometer. The jelly should be heated to 105°C/220°F.

8 Remove the pan from the heat, then skim any froth from the surface of the jelly using a slotted spoon.

9 Carefully remove the last traces of froth using a piece of kitchen paper. Pot the jelly immediately because it will start to set fairly quickly.

10 Cover and seal the jelly while it is hot, then leave to cool completely. (Do not move or tilt the jars until the jelly is completely cold and set.) Label the jars and store in a cool, dark place.

USING A JELLY BAG

Jelly bags, which are made from heavy-duty calico, cotton flannel or close-weave nylon, allow only the juice from the fruit to flow through, leaving the skins, pulp and pips (seeds) inside the bag. The fruit pulp and juices are very heavy, so strong tape or loops are positioned on the corners for hanging the bag securely on a stand, upturned stool or chair.

1 Before use, sterilize the jelly bag by scalding in boiling water. This process also helps the juices to run through the bag, rather than being absorbed into it.

2 If you don't have a jelly bag, you can use three or four layers of sterilized muslin (cheesecloth) or a piece of fine linen cloth instead. Simply line a large nylon or stainless-steel sieve with the muslin or linen.

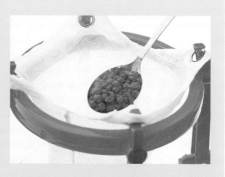

3 Carefully suspend the jelly bag or lined sieve over a large bowl to catch the juice. Make sure the bag or sieve is secure before spooning some of the simmered fruit and juices into it. (Don't add too much to start with.)

4 Leave the fruit to drain for a while, then spoon in more fruit. Continue gradually adding fruit in this way until it has all been placed in the bag or sieve, then leave to drain until it stops dripping completely. Some fruit will take 2–3 hours to release all their juice, while others may take as long as 12 hours.

5 Immediately after use, wash the jelly bag thoroughly, then rinse several times to remove all traces of detergent. Ensure the bag is completely dry before storing. The jelly bag may be reused many times, but be sure to sterilize it before every use.

boiling fruit twice

Rather than discarding the fruit pulp from the jelly bag after draining, you can boil it again to extract more liquid and flavour. This should be done only with pectin-rich fruits such as sharp apples, damsons or currants. The resulting jelly may have a slightly less concentrated flavour than jelly made from juice obtained from fruit that has been boiled once.

To boil the fruit a second time, return the fruit pulp to the pan and add just enough cold water to cover, using no more than half the amount of water used for the first boiling. Simmer the fruit gently for about 20 minutes, then drain through the jelly bag as before. Add the juice to the first batch.

flavouring jelly

Savoury jellies are often flavoured with fresh herbs such as thyme, mint, sage and rosemary. In some, such as mint jelly, the herb is most important and the fruit provides a base in which to suspend the herb; in others, herbs are used in small quantities to impart a subtle flavour.

1 To simply add flavour, add sprigs of herbs at the beginning of cooking. Woody herbs should be removed before draining because stems may damage the jelly bag.

2 When adding finely chopped herbs to the finished jelly, even distribution can be difficult and, if the jelly is too hot, the pieces may float to the top. To overcome this problem, put the herbs in a sieve and sprinkle with a little water to dampen them.

3 Leave the jelly to stand until it just starts to form a thin skin on top, then quickly stir in the chopped herbs. Pot straight away in very warm, but not hot, sterilized jars and seal. Cool before labelling.

4 Herb sprigs and aromatic leaves, such as lemon verbena or geranium leaves, can look stunning set in jelly. Pour the jelly into sterilized jars, then leave until semi-set and insert the herb sprigs or leaves.

TOP TIPS FOR SUCCESSFUL JELLY-MAKING

• There is no need to peel or stone (pit) fruit before cooking because all the debris will be removed during straining. However, it is important to discard any bruised or mouldy parts of the fruit because these will spoil the flavour. Rinse the fruit only if dusty or dirty.

• If using fruits such as apples that require longer cooking, chop the fruit very finely to reduce the cooking time required. Cooking the fruit for a shorter time also helps to give the jelly an intense, fresh flavour.

• Simmer the fruit very gently to extract the maximum amount of pectin and to avoid evaporating too much liquid. When cooking hard fruits that take a long time to soften, cover the pan for the first half of the cooking time to reduce the amount of liquid lost.

• Some fruits such as redcurrants or blackcurrants can be cooked in the oven to make highly flavoured jellies. Place the fruit in an oven-proof dish with about 75ml/5 tbsp water, cover tightly and cook at 140°C/275°F/Gas 1 for about 50 minutes, stirring occasionally, until pulpy. Drain through a jelly bag, then add 425g/15oz/generous 2 cups sugar for every 600ml/1 pint/2½ cups strained juice.

• Jellies set very quickly, so pot immediately. Warm a stainless steel funnel in the oven, or rinse a plastic one under hot water and dry it, then use to pot the jelly. If the jelly starts to set in the pan, warm it briefly until liquid again.

• Gently tap the jars as you fill with jelly to remove air bubbles.

• Although you can add a little butter to jam to disperse any scum, do not do this with jelly – it will make it cloudy.

MAKING MARMALADE

This preserve consists of a jelly base, usually with small pieces of fruit suspended in it. The name marmalade is derived from the Portuguese word *marmelo*, meaning quince, and it was from this fruit that marmalades were first made.

Modern marmalades are usually made from citrus fruits, or citrus fruits combined with other fruits such as pineapple, or flavoured with aromatic spices. Marmalades can range from thick and dark to light and translucent.

The citrus peel is shredded and cooked with the fruit juices and water until soft and tender, then boiled with sugar to make the marmalade. Citrus peel requires long, slow cooking in a large amount of water to become soft. The pith of Seville oranges, lemons and grapefruits becomes clear when cooked, but that of sweet oranges does not, so the pith should be scraped off the rind before shredding and cooking.

As well as classic marmalade, there is also jelly marmalade. This is perfect for people who enjoy the flavour of marmalade but do not like the peel that is suspended in the jelly. Rather than adding the shredded rind to the juices and water in the pan, the rind is tied in a muslin (cheesecloth) bag to keep it separate. The juices are then strained and boiled to setting point. The jelly may be left plain and potted as it is, or a little of the shredded rind can be stirred into the jelly just before potting. As with any jelly, it is difficult to give an exact yield for jelly marmalade.

making seville orange marmalade

Bitter Seville oranges are very popular for marmalade-making.

Makes about 2.5kg/5½lb

INGREDIENTS

900g/2lb Seville oranges

1 large lemon

2.4 litres/4 pints/2 quarts water

1.8kg/4lb/generous 9 cups preserving or granulated sugar

1 Wash and dry the fruits. If you are using waxed oranges and lemons, scrub the skins gently.

2 Halve the fruits and squeeze out the juice and pips (seeds), then pour into a muslin- (cheesecloth-) lined sieve set over a bowl.

3 Remove some of the pith from the citrus peels and reserve, then cut the peel into narrow strips.

4 Add the reserved pith to the pips in the muslin and tie together to make a loose bag. Allow plenty of room so that the water can bubble through the bag and extract the pectin from the pith and pips.

5 Place the shredded peel, juices and the muslin bag in a large preserving pan and pour in the water. Using a clean ruler, measure the depth of the contents in the pan and make a note of it.

6 Slowly bring the mixture to the boil and simmer for 1½–2 hours, or until the peel is very soft and the contents have reduced by about half their depth.

COOK'S TIPS

• To save time, shred the citrus peel in a food processor rather than by hand. Use either the fine or coarse cutting attachment.

• If you can't find Seville oranges, use Temple oranges instead.

7 To check that the peel is cooked, remove a piece from the pan and leave for a few minutes to cool. Once cooled, press the peel between finger and thumb; it should feel very soft.

8 Using a slotted spoon, remove the muslin bag from the pan and set it aside until cool enough to handle. Squeeze as much liquid as possible back into the pan to extract all the pectin from the pips and pith.

9 Add the sugar to the pan and stir over a low heat until the sugar has completely dissolved.

10 Bring the marmalade to the boil, then boil rapidly for about 10 minutes until setting point is reached (105°C/220°F). You may also use the flake or wrinkle test to check the set.

11 Using a slotted spoon, remove any scum from the surface of the marmalade, then leave to cool until a thin skin starts to form on the surface of the preserve.

12 Leave the marmalade to stand for about 5 minutes, then stir gently to distribute the peel evenly. Ladle into hot sterilized jars, then cover and seal.

making orange jelly marmalade

This recipe uses Seville oranges, and may be made as a plain jelly marmalade, or a few fine shreds of peel can be added before potting, which can look very pretty and adds an interesting texture. Any marmalade can be made in the same way; use exactly the same ingredients listed in the recipe but use the method below.

Makes about 2kg/4½lb

INGREDIENTS

450g/1lb Seville (Temple) oranges
1.75 litres/3 pints/7½ cups water
1.3kg/3lb/generous 6¾ cups preserving or granulated sugar
60ml/4 tbsp lemon juice

1 Wash and dry the oranges; gently scrub them with a soft brush if they have waxed skins.

2 If you want to add a little peel to the jelly marmalade, thinly pare and finely shred the rind from 2 or 3 of the oranges. Place the shreds in a square of muslin (cheesecloth) and tie it into a neat bag.

3 Halve the oranges and squeeze out the juice and pips (seeds), then tip the juice and pips into a large preserving pan.

4 Roughly chop the orange peel, including all the pith, and add it to the pan. Add the bag of shredded rind, if using, and pour over the water. Cover the pan with a lid and leave to soak for at least 4 hours, or overnight.

5 Bring the mixture to the boil, then reduce the heat and simmer gently for 1½ hours. Using a slotted spoon, remove the bag of peel, and carefully remove a piece of peel to check that it is tender. If not, re-tie the bag and simmer for a further 15–20 minutes. Remove the bag of peel and set aside.

6 Line a large nylon or stainless steel sieve with a double layer of muslin and place over a large bowl. Pour boiling water through the muslin to scald it. Discard the scalding water from the bowl. Alternatively, use a scalded jelly bag suspended over a bowl instead of the muslin-lined sieve.

7 Pour the fruit and juices into the sieve or jelly bag and leave to drain for at least 1 hour. Pour the juices into the cleaned pan.

8 Add the sugar, lemon juice and shredded orange rind, if using, to the pan. Stir over a low heat until the sugar has dissolved, then bring to the boil and boil rapidly for about 10 minutes until setting point is reached (105°C/220°F).

9 Remove any scum from the surface. Leave to cool until a thin skin starts to form on the surface. Stir, then pot, cover and seal.

TOP TIPS FOR SUCCESSFUL MARMALADE-MAKING

• Always wash citrus fruit well. Most citrus fruits have a wax coating that helps to prolong the life of the fruit, which should be removed before making the fruit into marmalade. Alternatively, buy unwaxed fruit, but always rinse before use.

• When shredding peel, always slice it slightly thinner than required in the finished preserve because the rind will swell slightly during cooking.

• Coarse-cut peel will take longer to soften than finely shredded peel. To reduce cooking time, soak the peel for a few hours in the water and juices before cooking.

• If the fruit needs to be peeled, put it in a bowl of boiling water and leave to stand for a couple of minutes. This will help to loosen the skins and make peeling easier. The rind's flavour will leach into the water, so use the soaking water in place of some of the measured water.

• If using small, thin-skinned fruit such as limes, cut the fruit into quarters lengthways, then slice flesh and rind into thin or thick shreds. If using larger, thick-skinned fruit such as grapefruit, pare off the peel, including some white pith, and shred. Cut the fruit into quarters, remove the remaining white pith and roughly chop the flesh.

• To make a coarse-cut preserve, boil the whole fruit for 2 hours until soft; pierce with a skewer to test. Lift out the fruit, halve, prise out the pips, then tie them loosely in muslin (cheesecloth) and add to the hot water. Boil rapidly for 10 minutes, then remove the bag. Slice the fruit and return to the pan. Stir in the sugar until dissolved, then boil to setting point.

• Shredded peel should be simmered gently; fierce cooking can give a tough result. Check that the peel is really soft before adding the sugar because it will not tenderize further after this.

• For easy removal, tie the muslin bag of pith and pips with string and attach it to the pan handle. It can then be lifted out of the boiling mixture easily.

• If the fruit contains a lot of pith, put only a small amount in the muslin bag with the pips. Put the remaining pith in a small pan, cover with water and boil for 10 minutes. Strain the liquid and use in place of some of the measured water for the recipe.

• To flavour marmalade with liqueur or spirits, add 15–30ml/ 1–2 tbsp for every 450g/1lb/ 2¼ cups sugar – stir it in just before potting. Unsweetened apple juice or dry (hard) cider may be used to replace up to half the water to add flavour to marmalades made with sharper fruits such as kumquats.

FRUIT CURDS, BUTTERS AND CHEESES

These rich, creamy preserves were once the highlight of an English tea during Edwardian and Victorian times. Curds and butters are delicious spread on slices of fresh bread and butter, or used as fillings for cakes; firmer fruit cheeses are usually sliced and can be enjoyed in similar ways. Fruit cheeses and butters are also very good served with roast meat, game or cheese.

Curds are made from fruit juice or purée cooked with eggs and butter. They have a soft texture and short keeping qualities. Fruit butters and cheeses are made from fruit purée boiled with sugar and are good if you have a glut of fruit because they require a relatively high proportion of fruit. Butters are lower in sugar and cooked for a shorter time, producing a soft, fruity preserve with a short shelf-life. Cheeses have a firm texture and may be set in moulds and turned out to serve.

MAKING FRUIT CURDS

Fruit curds are usually made with the juice of citrus fruits, but other acidic fruits such as passion fruit may be used. Smooth purées made from, for example, cooking apples or gooseberries can also be used.

The juice or purée is heated with eggs, butter and sugar until thick. The mixture is always cooked in a double boiler or a bowl set over a pan of simmering water to prevent the eggs curdling. Whole eggs are generally used, but if there is a lot of juice, egg yolks or a combination of whole eggs and yolks give a thicker result.

making lime curd

Makes about 675g/1½lb

INGREDIENTS

5 large, ripe juicy limes
115g/4oz/½ cup butter, cubed, at room temperature
350g/12oz/scant 1¾ cups caster (superfine) sugar
4 eggs, at room temperature

1 Finely grate the lime rind, ensuring you do not include any of the bitter white pith. Halve the limes and squeeze out the juice.

2 Place the lime rind in a large heatproof bowl set over a pan of barely simmering water, then strain in the lime juice to remove any bits of fruit or pips (seeds).

3 Add the cubed butter and the sugar to the bowl. Heat gently, stirring frequently, until the butter melts; the mixture should be barely warm, not hot.

4 Lightly beat the eggs with a fork, then strain through a fine sieve into the warm fruit mixture.

5 Keeping the water at a very gentle simmer, stir the fruit mixture continuously until the curd is thick enough to coat the back of a wooden spoon. Do not overcook because the curd will thicken on cooling.

6 Spoon the curd into warmed sterilized jars, then cover and seal when cold. Store in a cool, dark place, ideally in the refrigerator. Use within 2 months.

MAKING FRUIT BUTTERS

Smoother and thicker than jam, fruit butters have a spreadable quality not unlike dairy butter. Many recipes also contain a small amount of butter.

making apricot butter

Makes about 1.3kg/3lb

INGREDIENTS

1.3kg/3lb fresh ripe apricots
1 large orange
about 450ml/¾ pint/scant 2 cups water
about 675g/1½lb/scant 3½ cups caster (superfine) sugar
15g/½oz/1 tbsp butter (optional)

1 Rinse the apricots, then halve, stone (pit) and roughly chop. Remove the skins, unless you are going to purée the fruit by pressing through a sieve.

2 Scrub the orange and thinly pare 2–3 large strips of rind, avoiding any pith. Squeeze out the juice and put the apricots and the orange rind and juice in a large heavy pan.

3 Pour over enough of the water to cover the fruit. Bring to the boil, half-cover, then reduce the heat and simmer for 45 minutes.

jams and conserves

Preserving fruits in jams and conserves is one of the best ways of enjoying their delicious flavour all year round. In summer, with its long, warm days, there is an abundance of sweet juicy berries, while the autumn harvest offers a fabulous choice of stone and hedgerow fruits. All of these can be made into irresistible jams that can be enjoyed at any time of day – spread on toast, used as a filling or topping for plain cakes, or spooned over ice cream for a treat. All the recipes in this chapter will keep for at least 6 months.

seedless raspberry and passion fruit jam

The pips in raspberry jam can often put people off this wonderful preserve. This version has none of the pips and all of the flavour, and is enhanced by the tangy addition of passion fruit.

Makes about 1.3kg/3lb

INGREDIENTS

1.6kg/3½lb/14 cups raspberries

4 passion fruit, halved

1.3kg/3lb/6½ cups preserving sugar
with pectin, warmed

juice of 1 lemon

COOK'S TIPS

• Check the instructions on the sugar
packet for details of the boiling time.

• If you cannot find preserving sugar
with pectin, use the same quantity of
regular sugar and add powdered or
liquid pectin. Check the instructions
on the packet for quantities.

1 Place the raspberries in a large
pan, then scoop out the passion
fruit seeds and pulp and add to the
raspberries. Cover and cook over
a low heat for 20 minutes, or until
the juices begin to run.

2 Remove the pan from the heat
and leave to cool slightly, then,
using the back of a spoon, press
the fruit through a coarse sieve
into a preserving pan.

3 Add the sugar and lemon juice to
the pan and stir over a low heat
until the sugar has dissolved. Bring
to the boil and cook for 4 minutes,
or until the jam reaches setting
point (105°C/220°F).

4 Remove the pan from the heat
and skim off any scum. Leave to
cool slightly, then pour into
warmed sterilized jars. Seal and
label, then store in a cool place.

wild strawberry and rose petal conserve

This fragrant jam is ideal served with summer cream teas. Rose water complements the strawberries beautifully, but only add a few drops because the flavour can easily become over-powering.

Makes about 900g/2lb

INGREDIENTS

900g/2lb/8 cups wild Alpine
  strawberries

450g/1lb/4 cups strawberries, hulled
  and mashed

2 dark pink rose buds, petals only

juice of 2 lemons

1.3kg/3lb/6½ cups granulated
  sugar, warmed

a few drops of rose water

1 Put all the strawberries in a non-metallic bowl with the rose petals, lemon juice and warmed sugar. Cover and leave overnight.

2 The next day, tip the fruit into a preserving pan and heat gently, stirring, until all the sugar has dissolved. Boil for 10–15 minutes, or to setting point (105°C/220°F).

3 Stir the rose water into the jam, then remove the pan from the heat. Skim off any scum and leave to cool for 5 minutes, then stir and pour into warmed sterilized jars. Seal and label, then store.

COOK'S TIPS

• If you are unable to find wild berries, just use ordinary strawberries instead. Leave the smaller berries whole but mash any large ones.

• To make plain strawberry jam, make in the same way but leave out the rose petals and rose water.

cherry-berry conserve

Tart cranberries enliven the taste of cherries and also add an essential dose of pectin to this pretty conserve, which is fabulous spread on crumpets or toast. It is also delicious stirred into meaty gravies and sauces served with roast duck, poultry or pork.

2 Add the water to the pan. Cover and bring to the boil, then simmer for 20–30 minutes, or until the cranberries are very tender.

3 Add the sugar to the pan and heat gently, stirring, until the sugar has dissolved. Bring to the boil, then cook for 10 minutes, or to setting point (105°C/220°F).

4 Remove the pan from the heat and skim off any scum using a slotted spoon. Leave to cool for 10 minutes, then stir gently and pour into warmed sterilized jars. Seal, label and store.

Makes about 1.3kg/3lb

INGREDIENTS

350g/12oz/3 cups fresh cranberries

1kg/2¼lb/5½ cups cherries, pitted

120ml/4fl oz/½ cup blackcurrant
  or raspberry syrup

juice of 2 lemons

250ml/8fl oz/1 cup water

1.3kg/3lb/6½ cups preserving
  or granulated sugar, warmed

COOK'S TIP

The cranberries must be cooked until very tender before the sugar is added, otherwise they will become tough.

1 Put the cranberries in a food processor and process until coarsely chopped. Scrape into a pan and add the cherries, fruit syrup and lemon juice.

peach and amaretto jam

Adding amaretto (almond liqueur) produces a luxurious jam that's perfect served on warm buttered toast or English muffins. You can use peach schnapps in place of the amaretto if you prefer.

Makes about 1.3kg/3lb

INGREDIENTS

1.3kg/3lb peaches

250ml/8fl oz/1 cup water

juice of 2 lemons

1.3kg/3lb/6½ cups granulated
   sugar, warmed

45ml/3 tbsp amaretto liqueur

1 Carefully peel the peaches using a vegetable peeler, or blanch briefly in boiling water, then peel with a knife. Reserve the skins.

2 Halve and stone the fruit, dice the flesh and put in a pan with the water. Place the peach skins in a small pan with water to cover. Boil until the liquid is reduced to 30ml/2 tbsp. Press the skins and liquid through a sieve into the peaches. Cover and simmer for 20 minutes, or until soft.

3 Add the lemon juice and sugar to the pan. Heat, stirring, until the sugar has dissolved completely. Bring to the boil and cook for 10–15 minutes, or to setting point (105°C/220°F). Remove from the heat and skim off any scum from the surface using a slotted spoon.

4 Leave the jam to cool for about 10 minutes, then stir in the amaretto and pour into warmed sterilized jars. Seal, then leave to cool completely before labelling. Store in a cool, dark place.

gooseberry and elderflower jam

Pale green gooseberries and fragrant elderflowers make perfect partners in this sharp, aromatic, intensely flavoured jam. The jam turns an unexpected pink colour during cooking.

Makes about 2kg/4½lb

INGREDIENTS

1.3kg/3lb/12 cups firm gooseberries, topped and tailed

300ml/½ pint/1¼ cups water

1.3kg/3lb/6½ cups granulated sugar, warmed

juice of 1 lemon

2 handfuls of elderflowers removed from their stalks

COOK'S TIP

The time taken to reach setting point will vary depending on the ripeness of the gooseberries. The riper the fruit, the longer the jam will need to be cooked to reach setting point.

1 Put the gooseberries into a large preserving pan, add the water and bring the mixture to the boil.

2 Cover the pan with a lid and simmer gently for 20 minutes until the fruit is soft. Using a potato masher, gently mash the fruit to crush it lightly.

3 Add the sugar, lemon juice and elderflowers to the pan and stir over a low heat until the sugar has dissolved. Boil for 10 minutes, or to setting point (105°C/220°F). Remove from the heat, skim off any scum and cool for 5 minutes, then stir. Pot and seal, then leave to cool before labelling.

damson jam

Dark, plump damsons used to only be found growing in the wild, but today they are available commercially. They produce a deeply coloured and richly flavoured jam that makes a delicious treat spread on toasted English muffins or warm crumpets at tea time.

Makes about 2kg/4½lb

INGREDIENTS

1kg/2¼lb damsons or wild plums

1.4 litres/2¼ pints/6 cups water

1kg/2¼lb/5 cups preserving or granulated sugar, warmed

COOK'S TIP

It is important to seal the jars as soon as you have filled them to ensure the jam remains sterile. However, you should then leave the jars to cool completely before labelling and storing them to avoid the risk of burns.

1 Put the damsons in a preserving pan and pour in the water. Bring to the boil. Reduce the heat and simmer gently until the damsons are soft, then stir in the sugar.

2 Bring the mixture to the boil, skimming off stones as they rise. Boil to setting point (105°C/220°F). Leave to cool for 10 minutes, then pot. Seal, then label and store when cool.

pineapple and passion fruit jelly

This exotic jelly has a wonderful warming glow to its taste and appearance. For the best-flavoured jelly, use a tart-tasting, not too ripe pineapple rather than a very ripe, sweet one.

Makes about 900g/2lb

INGREDIENTS

1 large pineapple, peeled, topped and tailed and coarsely chopped

4 passion fruit, halved, with seeds and pulp scooped out

900ml/1½ pints/3¾ cups water

about 900g/2lb/4½ cups preserving or granulated sugar, warmed

COOK'S TIP

For the best flavour, choose passion fruits with dark, wrinkled skins.

1 Place the pineapple and the passion fruit seeds and pulp in a large pan with the water.

2 Bring the mixture to the boil, cover and simmer for 1½ hours. Remove from the heat and leave to cool slightly. Transfer the fruit to a food processor and process briefly.

3 Tip the fruit pulp and any juices from the pan, into a scalded jelly bag suspended over a non-metallic bowl and leave to drain overnight.

4 Measure the strained juice into a preserving pan and add 450g/1lb/2¼ cups warmed sugar for every 600ml/1 pint/2½ cups juice.

5 Heat gently, stirring, until the sugar has dissolved. Increase the heat and boil rapidly, without stirring, for 10–15 minutes or to setting point (105°C/220°F).

6 Remove the pan from the heat and skim off any scum using a slotted spoon. Ladle the jelly into warmed sterilized jars, cover and seal. When cool, label and store in a cool, dark place.

pomegranate and grenadine jelly

*The slightly tart flavoured, jewel-like flesh of the pomegranate makes the most wonderful jelly.
Be careful though, because pomegranate juice can stain indelibly when spilt on clothing.*

Makes about 900g/2lb

INGREDIENTS

6 ripe red pomegranates, peeled and
  seeds removed from membranes

120ml/4fl oz/½ cup grenadine syrup

juice and pips (seeds) of 2 oranges

300ml/½ pint/1¼ cups water

about 900g/2lb/4½ cups preserving
  or granulated sugar, warmed

1 Put the pomegranate seeds in
bowl and crush to release their
juice. Transfer them to a pan and
add the grenadine, orange juice,
pips and water.

2 Bring the mixture to the boil,
cover and simmer for 1½ hours.
Mash the fruit and leave to cool
slightly, then pour into a scalded
jelly bag suspended over a bowl
and leave to drain overnight.

3 Measure the juice into a pan and
add 450g/1lb/2¼ cups sugar for
every 600ml/1 pint/2½ cups juice.

4 Heat, stirring, over a low heat
until the sugar has dissolved.
Increase the heat and boil rapidly,
without stirring, for 5–10 minutes,
or until the jelly reaches setting
point (105°C/220°F).

5 Remove the pan from the heat
and skim off any scum. Ladle into
warmed sterilized jars, cover, seal
and label. Store in a cool place.

marmalades

These classic preserves come somewhere between a jam and a jelly and are traditionally served for breakfast. Usually made of citrus fruits, marmalades have a jelly base with small pieces of fruit suspended in it. They can be tart and bitter with thick cut shreds of peel, or sweet with thinly cut zest. The Seville orange is favoured because of its refreshing tang and high pectin content but any citrus fruit can be used, as long as its shredded rind is cooked until very tender.

oxford marmalade

The characteristic caramel colour and rich flavour of a traditional Oxford marmalade is obtained by cutting the fruit coarsely and cooking it for several hours before adding the sugar.

Makes about 2.25kg/5lb

INGREDIENTS

900g/2lb Seville (Temple) oranges

1.75 litres/3 pints/7½ cups water

1.3kg/3lb/6½ cups granulated sugar, warmed

COOK'S TIP

Traditionalist say that only bitter oranges such as Seville should be used to make marmalade. Although this isn't always true, it is most certainly the case when making Oxford marmalade.

1 Scrub the orange skins, then remove the rind using a vegetable peeler. Thickly slice the rind and put in a large pan.

2 Chop the fruit, reserving the pips (seeds), and add to the rind in the pan, along with the water. Tie the orange pips in a piece of muslin (cheesecloth) and add to the pan. Bring to the boil, then cover and simmer for 2 hours. Add more water during cooking to maintain the same volume. Remove the pan from the heat and leave overnight.

3 The next day, remove the muslin bag from the oranges, squeezing well, and return the pan to the heat. Bring to the boil, then cover and simmer for 1 hour.

4 Add the warmed sugar to the pan, then slowly bring the mixture to the boil, stirring until the sugar has dissolved completely. Increase the heat and boil rapidly for about 15 minutes, or until setting point is reached (105°C/220°F).

5 Remove the pan from the heat and skim off any scum from the surface. Leave to cool for about 5 minutes, stir, then pour into warmed sterilized jars and seal. When cold, label, then store in a cool, dark place.

st clement's marmalade

This classic preserve made from oranges and lemons has a lovely citrus tang. It has a light, refreshing flavour and is perfect for serving for breakfast, spread on freshly toasted bread.

Makes about 2.25kg/5lb

INGREDIENTS

450g/1lb Seville (Temple) oranges

450g/1lb sweet oranges

4 lemons

1.5 litres/2½ pints/6¼ cups water

1.2kg/2½lb/5½ cups granulated sugar, warmed

1 Wash the oranges and lemons, then halve and squeeze the juice into a large pan. Tie the pips (seeds) and membranes in a muslin (cheesecloth) bag, shred the orange and lemon rind and add to the pan.

2 Add the water to the pan, bring to the boil, then cover and simmer for 2 hours. Remove the muslin bag, leave to cool, then squeeze any liquid back into the pan.

3 Add the warmed sugar to the pan and stir over a low heat until completely dissolved. Bring to the boil and boil rapidly for about 15 minutes or until the marmalade reaches setting point (105°C/220°F).

4 Remove the pan from the heat and skim off any scum from the surface. Leave to cool for about 5 minutes, stir, then pour into warmed sterilized jars and seal. When cold, label, then store in a cool, dark place.

pink grapefruit and cranberry marmalade

Cranberries give this glorious marmalade an extra tartness and a full fruit flavour, as well as an inimitable vibrant colour. The resulting preserve makes a lively choice for breakfast or a brilliant accompaniment for cold roast turkey during the festive season.

2 Tie the grapefruit and lemon pips in a muslin (cheesecloth) bag and place in a large pan with the grapefruit slices and lemon juice.

3 Add the water and bring to the boil. Cover and simmer gently for 1½–2 hours, or until the grapefruit rind is very tender. Remove the muslin bag, leave to cool, then squeeze over the pan.

4 Add the cranberries to the pan, then bring to the boil. Simmer for 15–20 minutes, or until the berries have popped and softened.

Makes about 2.25kg/5lb

5 Add the sugar to the pan and stir over a low heat until the sugar has completely dissolved. Bring to the boil and boil rapidly for about 10 minutes, or until setting point is reached (105°C/220°F).

INGREDIENTS

675g/1½lb pink grapefruit
juice and pips (seeds) of 2 lemons
900ml/1½ pints/3¾ cups water
225g/8oz/2 cups cranberries
1.3kg/3lb/6½ cups granulated sugar, warmed

6 Remove the pan from the heat and skim off any scum from the surface using a slotted spoon. Leave to cool for 5–10 minutes, then stir and pour into warmed sterilized jars. Seal, then label when the marmalade is cold.

COOK'S TIP

You can use fresh or frozen cranberries to make this marmalade. Either gives equally good results.

1 Wash, halve and quarter the grapefruit, then slice them thinly, reserving the pips (seeds) and any juice that runs out.

curds, butters and cheeses

These smooth, thick, luscious preserves capture the colours and flavours of the season. Butters and curds are thick and spreadable, delicious spooned on to toast or griddle cakes. In contrast, cheeses are firmer and can be cut into wedges or slices, or set in small individual moulds. Serve them as a delicious accompaniment to roast meats or dairy cheeses, or cut into wedges, dredge in sugar and serve as a sweetmeat after the meal.

lemon curd

This classic tangy, creamy curd is still one of the most popular of all the curds. It is delicious spread thickly over freshly baked white bread or served with American-style pancakes, and also makes a wonderfully rich, zesty sauce spooned over fresh fruit tarts.

Makes about 450g/1lb

INGREDIENTS

3 lemons

200g/7oz/1 cup caster (superfine) sugar

115g/4oz/8 tbsp unsalted (sweet) butter, diced

2 large (US extra large) eggs

2 large (US extra large) egg yolks

1 Wash the lemons, then finely grate the rind and place in a large heatproof bowl. Using a sharp knife, halve the lemons and squeeze the juice into the bowl. Set over a pan of gently simmering water and add the sugar and butter. Stir until the sugar has dissolved and the butter melted.

2 Put the eggs and yolks in a bowl and beat together with a fork. Pour the eggs through a sieve into the lemon mixture, and whisk well until thoroughly combined.

3 Stir the mixture constantly over the heat until the lemon curd thickens and lightly coats the back of a wooden spoon.

4 Remove the pan from the heat and pour the curd into small, warmed sterilized jars. Cover, seal and label. Store in a cool, dark place, ideally in the refrigerator. Use within 3 months. (Once opened, store in the refrigerator.)

COOK'S TIP

If you are really impatient when it comes to cooking, it is possible to cook the curd in a heavy pan directly over a low heat. However, you really need to watch it like a hawk to avoid the mixture curdling. If the curd looks as though it's beginning to curdle, plunge the base of the pan in cold water and beat vigorously.

seville orange curd

Using flavoursome Seville oranges gives this curd a fantastic orange flavour and a real citrus tang. It is perfect for spreading on toast for breakfast or at tea time, and is also superlative folded into whipped cream and used as a filling for cakes, roulades and scones.

Makes about 450g/1lb

INGREDIENTS

2 Seville (Temple) oranges

115g/4oz/8 tbsp unsalted (sweet) butter, diced

200g/7oz/1 cup caster (superfine) sugar

2 large (US extra large) eggs

2 large (US extra large) egg yolks

1 Wash the oranges, then finely grate the rind and place in a large heatproof bowl. Halve the oranges and squeeze the juice into the bowl with the rind.

2 Place the bowl over a pan of gently simmering water and add the butter and sugar. Stir until the sugar has completely dissolved and the butter melted.

3 Put the eggs and yolks in a small bowl and lightly whisk, then pour into the orange mixture through a sieve. Whisk them together until thoroughly combined.

4 Stir the orange and egg mixture constantly over the heat until the mixture thickens and lightly coats the back of a wooden spoon.

5 Pour the orange curd into small, warmed sterilized jars, cover and seal. Store in a cool, dark place, preferably in the refrigerator.

WATCHPOINTS

• The very young, the elderly, pregnant women, and those with a compromised immune system are advised against eating raw eggs or food containing raw eggs. Although the eggs in fruit curds are lightly cooked, they may still be unsuitable for these groups of people.

• Fruit curds do not have the shelf-life of many other preserves and should be used within 3 months of making.

• Once opened, always store fruit curds in the refrigerator.

grapefruit curd

If you favour tangy and refreshing preserves, this grapefruit curd is the one to try. Really fresh free-range eggs give the best results and flavour when making curd.

Makes about 675g/1½lb

INGREDIENTS

finely grated rind and juice of 1 grapefruit

115g/4oz/8 tbsp unsalted (sweet)
  butter, diced

200g/7oz/1 cup caster (superfine) sugar

4 large (US extra large) eggs,
  lightly beaten

1 Put the grapefruit rind and juice in a large heatproof bowl with the butter and sugar, and set over a pan of gently simmering water. Heat the mixture, stirring occasionally, until the sugar has dissolved and the butter melted.

2 Add the beaten eggs to the fruit mixture, straining them through a sieve. Whisk together, then stir constantly over the heat until the mixture thickens and lightly coats the back of a wooden spoon.

3 Pour the curd into small, warmed sterilized jars, cover and seal. Label when the jars are cold. Store in a cool, dark place, preferably in the refrigerator and use within 3 months. (Once opened, store the curd in the refrigerator.)

VARIATION

Tangy grapefruit and sweet orange marry particularly well in creamy fruit curds. Add the grated rind of a small orange to this grapefruit recipe for an extra zingy, zesty alternative.

spiced cherry cheese

For the best results, try to use cherries that have a good tart flavour and dark red flesh.
Serve as an accompaniment to strong cheese, or sliced with roast duck or pork.

Makes about 900g/2lb

INGREDIENTS

1.5kg/3lb 6oz/8¼ cups cherries,
  stoned (pitted)

2 cinnamon sticks

800g/1¾lb/4 cups granulated
  sugar, warmed

COOK'S TIPS

• Store the cheese in a cool, dark place for 2–3 months before eating.

• To serve a fruit cheese in slices, turn it out of its container and slice using a sharp knife. The slices may be cut into smaller portions. Try to use a straight-sided container so that the cheese can slide out easily.

1 Place the cherries in a large pan with the cinnamon sticks. Pour in enough water to almost cover the fruit. Bring to the boil, then cover and simmer for 20–30 minutes, or until the cherries are very tender. Remove the cinnamon sticks from the pan and discard.

2 Tip the fruit into a sieve and press into a bowl, using the back of a spoon. Measure the purée into a large, heavy pan, adding 350g/12oz/1¾ cups warmed sugar for every 600ml/1 pint/2½ cups purée.

3 Gently heat the purée, stirring, until the sugar dissolves. Increase the heat and cook for 45 minutes, stirring frequently, until very thick. To test, spoon a little of the cheese on to a cold plate; it should form a firm jelly.

4 Spoon into warmed, sterilized jars or oiled moulds. Seal, label, and store in a cool, dark place.

blackberry and apple cheese

This rich, dark preserve has an incredibly intense flavour and fabulous colour. For a fragrant twist, add a few raspberries – or even strawberries – in place of some of the blackberries.

Makes about 900g/2lb

INGREDIENTS

900g/2lb/8 cups blackberries

450g/1lb tart cooking apples, cut into chunks, with skins and cores intact

grated rind and juice of 1 lemon

800g/1¾lb/4 cups granulated sugar, warmed

1 Put the blackberries, apples and lemon rind and juice in a pan and pour in enough water to come halfway up the fruit. Bring to the boil, then uncover and simmer for 15–20 minutes or until the fruit is very soft.

2 Leave the fruit to cool slightly, then tip the mixture into a sieve and press into a bowl, using the back of a spoon. Measure the purée into a large, heavy pan, adding 400g/14oz/2 cups warmed sugar for every 600ml/1 pint/2½ cups purée.

3 Gently heat the purée, stirring, until the sugar dissolves. Increase the heat slightly and cook for 40–50 minutes, stirring frequently, until very thick (see Cook's Tip).

4 Spoon the blackberry and apple cheese into warmed, sterilized straight-sided jars or oiled moulds. Seal and label the jars or moulds, then store in a cool, dark place for 2–3 months to dry out slightly.

COOK'S TIP

When the cheese is ready, you should be able to see the base of the pan when a wooden spoon is drawn through the mixture. Spoon a small amount of the mixture on to a chilled plate; it should form a firm jelly.

sweet fruit preserves

Seasonal fruits bottled in spirits or syrups look stunning stacked in your store cupboard and taste divine spooned over ice cream, cakes and desserts. Some fruits can even be enjoyed on their own with just a spoonful of cream. Preserving in syrups and alcohol helps to retain the colour, texture and flavour of the fruit, while ensuring that they do not ferment or spoil on keeping. Alcohol also adds extra flavour and body and can turn simple preserved fruits into an indulgent treat.

mulled pears

These pretty pears in a warming spiced syrup make a tempting dessert, particularly during the cold winter months. Serve them with crème fraîche or vanilla ice cream, or in open tarts.

Makes about 1.3kg/3lb

INGREDIENTS

1.8kg/4lb small firm pears

1 orange

1 lemon

2 cinnamon sticks, halved

12 whole cloves

5cm/2in piece fresh root ginger, peeled and sliced

300g/11oz/1½ cups granulated sugar

1 bottle fruity light red wine

COOK'S TIP

Pears have a delicate flavour, so use a light, fruity wine such as Beaujolais or Merlot to make the syrup.

1 Peel the pears leaving the stalks intact. Peel very thin strips of rind from the orange and lemon, using a vegetable peeler. Pack the pears and citrus rind into large sterilized preserving jars, dividing the spices evenly between the jars.

2 Preheat the oven to 120°C/250°F/Gas ½. Put the sugar and wine in a large pan and heat gently, stirring, until the sugar has completely dissolved. Bring the mixture to the boil, then cook for 5 minutes.

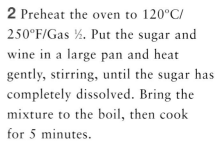

3 Pour the wine syrup over the pears, making sure that there are no air pockets and that the fruits are completely covered with the syrup.

4 Cover the jars with their lids, but do not seal. Place them in the oven and cook for 2½–3 hours.

5 Carefully remove the jars from the oven, place on a dry dishtowel and seal. Leave the jars to cool completely, then label and store in a cool, dark place.

COOK'S TIP

To check that jars are properly sealed, leave them to cool for 24 hours, then loosen the clasp. Very carefully, try lifting the jar by the lid alone: if the jar is sealed properly, the lid should be fixed firmly enough to take the weight of the pot. Replace the clasp and store until ready to use.

rumtopf

This fruit preserve originated in Germany, where special earthenware rumtopf pots are traditionally filled with fruits as they come into season. It is not necessary to use the specific pot; you can use a large preserving jar instead. Store in a cool, dark place.

Makes about 3 litres/5 pints/12½ cups

INGREDIENTS

900g/2lb fruit, such as strawberries, blackberries, blackcurrants, redcurrants, peaches, apricots, cherries and plums

250g/9oz/1¼ cups granulated sugar

1 litre/1¾ pints/4 cups white rum

1 Prepare the fruit: remove stems, skins, cores and stones (pits) and cut larger fruit into bitesize pieces. Combine the fruit and sugar in a large non-metallic bowl, cover and leave to stand for 30 minutes.

2 Spoon the fruit and juices into a sterilized 3 litre/5 pint/12½ cup preserving or earthenware jar and pour in the white rum to cover.

3 Cover the jar with clear film (plastic wrap), then seal and store in a cool, dark place.

4 As space allows, and as different fruits come into season, add more fruit, sugar and rum in appropriate proportions, as described above.

5 When the jar is full, store in a cool, dark place for 2 months. Serve the fruit spooned over ice cream or other desserts and enjoy the rum in glasses as a liqueur.

spiced apple mincemeat

This fruity mincemeat is traditionally used to fill little pies at Christmas but it is great at any time. Try it as a filling for large tarts finished with a lattice top and served with custard. To make a lighter mincemeat, add some extra grated apple just before using.

Makes about 1.8kg/4lb

INGREDIENTS

500g/1¼lb tart cooking apples, peeled, cored and finely diced

115g/4oz/½ cup ready-to-eat dried apricots, coarsely chopped

900g/2lb/5⅓ cups luxury dried mixed fruit

115g/4oz/1 cup whole blanched almonds, chopped

175g/6oz/1 cup shredded beef or vegetarian suet (chilled, grated shortening)

225g/8oz/generous 1 cup dark muscovado (molasses) sugar

grated rind and juice of 1 orange

grated rind and juice of 1 lemon

5ml/1 tsp ground cinnamon

2.5ml/½ tsp grated nutmeg

2.5ml/½ tsp ground ginger

120ml/4fl oz/½ cup brandy

1 Put the apples, apricots, dried fruit, almonds, suet and sugar in a large non-metallic bowl and stir together until thoroughly combined.

2 Add the orange and lemon rind and juice, cinnamon, nutmeg, ginger and brandy and mix well. Cover the bowl with a clean dishtowel and leave to stand in a cool place for 2 days, stirring occasionally.

3 Spoon the mincemeat into cool sterilized jars, pressing down well, and being very careful not to trap any air bubbles. Cover and seal.

4 Store the jars in a cool, dark place for at least 4 weeks before using. Once opened, store in the refrigerator and use within 4 weeks. Unopened, the mincemeat will keep for 1 year.

COOK'S TIP

If, when opened, the mincemeat seems dry, pour a little extra brandy or orange juice into the jar and gently stir in. You may need to remove a spoonful or two of the mincemeat from the jar to do this.

pickles

Sharp and sweet, warm and mellow, or hot and piquant – pickles are the magical condiments that can transform simple foods into exhilarating meals. Fresh fruits and vegetables preserved in salt or vinegar and flavoured with spices and herbs make fabulously flavoursome and aromatic accompaniments to cold meats and cheeses, and go well with many roast meats too. They are simple to make and gloriously varied – each one with its own unique character and taste.

dill pickles

Redolent of garlic and piquant with fresh chilli, salty dill pickles can be supple and succulent or crisp and crunchy. Every pickle aficionado has a favourite type.

Makes about 900g/2lb

INGREDIENTS

20 small, ridged or knobbly pickling
   (small) cucumbers
2 litres/3½ pints/8 cups water
175g/6oz/¾ cup coarse sea salt
15–20 garlic cloves, unpeeled
2 bunches fresh dill
15ml/1 tbsp dill seeds
30ml/2 tbsp mixed pickling spice
1 or 2 hot fresh chillies

1 Scrub the cucumbers and rinse well in cold water. Leave to dry.

2 Put the measured water and salt in a large pan and bring to the boil. Turn off the heat and leave to cool to room temperature.

3 Using the flat side of a knife blade or a wooden mallet, lightly crush each garlic clove, breaking the papery skin.

4 Pack the cucumbers tightly into one or two wide-necked, sterilized jars, layering them with the garlic, fresh dill, dill seeds and pickling spice. Add one chilli to each jar. Pour over the cooled brine, making sure that the cucumbers are completely covered. Tap the jars on the work surface to dispel any trapped air bubbles.

5 Cover the jars with lids and then leave to stand at room temperature for 4–7 days before serving. Store in the refrigerator.

COOK'S TIP

If you cannot find ridged or knobbly pickling cucumbers, use any kind of small cucumbers instead.

pickled mushrooms with garlic

This method of preserving mushrooms is popular throughout Europe. The pickle is good made with cultivated mushrooms, but it is worth including a couple of sliced ceps for their flavour.

Makes about 900g/2lb

INGREDIENTS

500g/1¼lb/8 cups mixed mushrooms, such as small ceps, chestnut mushrooms, shiitake and girolles

300ml/½ pint/1¼ cups white wine vinegar or cider vinegar

15ml/1 tbsp sea salt

5ml/1 tsp caster (superfine) sugar

300ml/½ pint/1¼ cups water

4–5 fresh bay leaves

8 large fresh thyme sprigs

15 garlic cloves, peeled, halved, with any green shoots removed

1 small red onion, halved and thinly sliced

2–3 small dried red chillies

5ml/1 tsp coriander seeds, lightly crushed

5ml/1 tsp black peppercorns

a few strips of lemon rind

250–350ml/8–12fl oz/1–1½ cups extra virgin olive oil

1 Trim and wipe the mushrooms and cut any large ones in half.

2 Put the vinegar, salt, sugar and water in a pan and bring to the boil. Add the bay leaves, thyme, garlic, onion, chillies, coriander seeds, peppercorns and lemon rind and simmer for 2 minutes.

3 Add the mushrooms to the pan and simmer for 3–4 minutes. Drain the mushrooms through a seive, retaining all the herbs and spices, then set aside for a few minutes more until the mushrooms are thoroughly drained.

4 Fill one large or two small cool sterilized jars with the mushrooms. Distribute the garlic, onion, herbs and spices evenly among the layers of mushrooms, then add enough olive oil to cover by at least 1cm/½in. You may need to use extra oil if you are making two jars.

5 Leave the pickle to settle, then tap the jars on the work surface to dispel any air bubbles. Seal the jars, then store in the refrigerator. Use within 2 weeks.

pickled red cabbage

This delicately spiced and vibrant-coloured pickle is an old-fashioned favourite to serve with bread and cheese for an informal lunch, or to use to accompany cold ham, duck or goose.

Makes about 1–1.6kg/2¼–3½lb

INGREDIENTS

675g/1½lb/6 cups red
  cabbage, shredded

1 large Spanish onion, sliced

30ml/2 tbsp sea salt

600ml/1 pint/2½ cups red wine vinegar

75g/3oz/6 tbsp light muscovado
  (brown) sugar

15ml/1 tbsp coriander seeds

3 cloves

2.5cm/1in piece fresh root ginger

1 whole star anise

2 bay leaves

4 eating apples

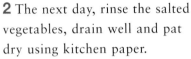

1 Put the cabbage and onion in a bowl, add the salt and mix well until thoroughly combined. Tip the mixture into a colander over a bowl and leave to drain overnight.

2 The next day, rinse the salted vegetables, drain well and pat dry using kitchen paper.

3 Pour the vinegar into a pan, add the sugar, spices and bay leaves and bring to the boil. Remove from the heat and leave to cool.

4 Core and chop the apples, then layer with the cabbage and onions in sterilized preserving jars. Pour over the cooled spiced vinegar. (If you prefer a milder pickle, strain out the spices first). Seal the jars and store for 1 week before eating. Eat within 2 months. Once opened, store in the refrigerator.

pickled turnips and beetroot

This delicious pickle is a Middle Eastern speciality. The turnips turn a rich red in their beetroot-spiked brine and look gorgeous stacked on shelves in the storecupboard.

2 Put the salt and water in a bowl, stir and leave to stand until the salt has completely dissolved.

3 Sprinkle the beetroot with lemon juice and place in the bottom of four 1.2 litre/2 pint sterilized jars. Top with sliced turnip, packing them in very tightly, then pour over the brine, making sure that the vegetables are covered.

4 Seal the jars and leave in a cool place for 7 days before serving.

Makes about 1.6kg/3½lb

INGREDIENTS

1kg/2¼lb young turnips
3–4 raw beetroot (beets)
about 45ml/3 tbsp coarse sea salt
about 1.5 litres/2½ pints/6¼ cups water
juice of 1 lemon

COOK'S TIP

Be careful when preparing the beetroot because their bright red juice can stain clothing.

1 Wash the turnips and beetroot, but do not peel them, then cut into slices about 5mm/¼in thick.

shallots in balsamic vinegar

These whole shallots, cooked in balsamic vinegar and herbs, are a modern variation on traditional pickled onions. They have a much more gentle, smooth flavour and are delicious served with cold meats or robustly flavoured hard cheeses.

Makes one large jar

INGREDIENTS

500g/1¼lb shallots

30ml/2 tbsp muscovado (molasses) sugar

several bay leaves and/or fresh thyme sprigs

300ml/½ pint/1¼ cups balsamic vinegar

VARIATION

Use other robust herbs in place of the thyme sprigs. Rosemary, oregano or marjoram are all good choices.

1 Put the unpeeled shallots in a bowl. Pour over boiling water and leave to stand for 2 minutes to loosen the skins. Drain and peel the shallots, leaving them whole.

2 Put the sugar, bay leaves and/or thyme and vinegar in a large heavy pan and bring to the boil. Add the shallots, cover and simmer gently for about 40 minutes, or until the shallots are just tender.

3 Transfer the shallots and vinegar mixture to a warmed sterilized jar, packing the shallots down well. Seal and label the jar, then store in a cool, dark place for about 1 month before eating.

hot thai pickled shallots

Although they may be quite difficult to find and require lengthy preparation, Thai pink shallots look and taste exquisite in this spiced pickle. The shallots taste good finely sliced, and served as a condiment with a wide range of South-east Asian meals.

Makes about three jars

INGREDIENTS

5–6 fresh red or green bird's eye chillies, halved and seeded if liked

500g/1¼lb Thai pink shallots, peeled

2 large garlic cloves, peeled, halved and green shoots removed

600ml/1 pint/2½ cups cider vinegar

45ml/3 tbsp granulated sugar

10ml/2 tsp salt

5cm/2in piece fresh root ginger, sliced

15ml/1 tbsp coriander seeds

2 lemon grass stalks, cut in half lengthways

4 kaffir lime leaves or strips of lime rind

15ml/1 tbsp chopped fresh coriander (cilantro)

1 If leaving the chillies whole (they will be hotter), prick several times with a cocktail stick (toothpick).

2 Bring a large pan of water to the boil. Blanch the chillies, shallots and garlic for 1–2 minutes, then drain. Rinse the vegetables under cold water and leave to drain.

VARIATION

Ordinary shallots and pickling onions are widely available and can be preserved using the same method.

3 To prepare the vinegar, put the cider vinegar, sugar, salt, ginger, coriander seeds, lemon grass and lime leaves or lime rind in a large pan and bring to the boil. Simmer over a low heat for 3–4 minutes, then remove from the heat and set aside to cool.

4 Using a slotted spoon, remove the sliced ginger from the pan and discard. Return the vinegar to the boil, then add the fresh coriander, garlic and chillies, and cook for about 1 minute.

5 Pack the shallots, spices and aromatics into warmed sterilized jars and pour over the hot vinegar. Cool, then seal. Leave in a dark place for 2 months before eating.

english pickled onions

These powerful pickles are traditionally served with a plate of cold meats and bread and cheese. They should be made with malt vinegar and stored for at least 6 weeks before eating.

Makes about four jars

INGREDIENTS

1kg/2¼lb pickling onions

115g/4oz/½ cup salt

750ml/1¼ pints/3 cups malt vinegar

15ml/1 tbsp sugar

2–3 dried red chillies

5ml/1 tsp brown mustard seeds

15ml/1 tbsp coriander seeds

5ml/1 tsp allspice berries

5ml/1 tsp black peppercorns

5cm/2in piece fresh root ginger, sliced

2–3 blades mace

2–3 fresh bay leaves

1 To peel the onions, trim off the root ends, but leave the onion layers attached. Cut a thin slice off the top (neck) end of the onion. Place the onions in a bowl, then cover with boiling water. Leave to stand for about 4 minutes, then drain. The skin should then be easy to peel using a small, sharp knife.

2 Place the peeled onions in a bowl and cover with cold water, then drain the water into a large pan. Add the salt and heat slightly to dissolve it, then cool before pouring the brine over the onions.

3 Place a plate inside the top of the bowl and weigh it down slightly so that it keeps all the onions submerged in the brine. Leave to stand for 24 hours.

4 Meanwhile, place the vinegar in a large pan. Wrap all the remaining ingredients, except the bay leaves, in a piece of muslin (cheesecloth). Bring to the boil, simmer for about 5 minutes, then remove the pan from the heat. Set aside and leave to infuse overnight.

5 The next day, drain the onions, rinse and pat dry. Pack them into sterilized 450g/1lb jars. Add some or all of the spice from the vinegar, except the ginger slices. The pickle will become hotter if you add the chillies. Pour the vinegar over to cover and add the bay leaves. (Store leftover vinegar in a bottle for another batch of pickles.)

6 Seal the jars with non-metallic lids and store in a cool, dark place for at least 6 weeks before eating.

instant pickle of mixed vegetables

This fresh, salad-style pickle doesn't need lengthy storing so makes the perfect choice if you need a bowl of pickle immediately. However, it does not have good storing properties.

Makes about 450g/1lb

INGREDIENTS

½ cauliflower head, cut into florets

2 carrots, sliced

2 celery sticks, thinly sliced

¼–½ white cabbage, thinly sliced

115g/4oz/scant 1 cup runner (green) beans, cut into bitesize pieces

6 garlic cloves, sliced

1–4 fresh chillies, whole or sliced

5cm/2in piece fresh root ginger, sliced

1 red (bell) pepper, sliced

2.5ml/½ tsp turmeric

105ml/7 tbsp white wine vinegar

15–30ml/1–2 tbsp granulated sugar

60–90ml/4–6 tbsp olive oil

juice of 2 lemons

salt

1 Toss the cauliflower, carrots, celery, cabbage, beans, garlic, chillies, ginger and pepper with salt and leave them to stand in a colander over a bowl for 4 hours.

2 Shake the vegetables well to remove any excess juices.

3 Transfer the salted vegetables to a bowl. Add the turmeric, vinegar, sugar to taste, oil and lemon juice. Toss to combine, then add enough water to distribute the flavours. Cover the bowl and leave to chill for at least 1 hour, or until you are ready to serve.

stuffed baby aubergines

This Middle Eastern fermented pickle makes a succulent and spicy accompaniment to cold meats, but is equally good served with a few salad leaves and bread as a simple appetizer.

Makes about 3 jars

INGREDIENTS

1kg/2¼lb baby aubergines (eggplant)
2 fresh red chillies, halved lengthways
2 green chillies, halved lengthways
2 celery sticks, cut into matchstick strips
2 carrots, cut into matchstick strips
4 garlic cloves, peeled and finely chopped
20ml/4 tsp salt
4 small fresh vine leaves (optional)
750ml/1¼ pints/3 cups cooled boiled water
45ml/3 tbsp white wine vinegar

1 Trim the aubergine stems, but do not remove them completely. Cut a slit lengthways along each aubergine, almost through to the other side, to make a pocket.

COOK'S TIPS

• Aubergines come in a multitude of colours from a deep purple-black to yellow and creamy white. Whichever type you use, choose ones with taut, glossy skins.
• Steam the aubergines as soon as you have slit them open because their flesh discolours rapidly when exposed to air.

2 Steam the slit aubergines for 5–6 minutes or until they are just tender when tested with the tip of a sharp knife.

3 Put the aubergines in a colander set over a bowl, then place a plate on top. Place a few weights on the plate to press it down gently and leave for 4 hours to squeeze out the moisture from the vegetables.

4 Finely chop two red and two green chilli halves and place in a bowl. Add the celery and carrots to the chillies with the garlic and 5ml/1 tsp of the salt. Mix and use to stuff the aubergine pockets.

5 Tightly pack the aubergines, remaining chillies and vine leaves, if using, into a large sterilized jar.

6 Pour the water into a jug (pitcher) and add the remaining 15ml/1 tbsp salt and the vinegar. Stir together until the salt has dissolved. Pour enough brine into the jar to cover the aubergines, then weigh down the top.

7 Cover the jar with a clean dishtowel and leave in a warm, well-ventilated place to ferment. The brine will turn cloudy as fermentation starts, but will clear after 1–2 weeks when the pickle has finished fermenting. As soon as this happens, cover and seal the jar and store in the refrigerator. Eat the pickle within 2 months.

preserved lemons

These richly flavoured fruits are widely used in Middle Eastern cooking. Only the rind, which contains the essential flavour of the lemon is used in recipes. Traditionally whole lemons are preserved, but this recipe uses wedges, which can be packed into jars more easily.

2 Pack the salted lemon wedges into two 1.2 litre/2 pint/5 cup warmed sterilized jars. To each jar, add 30–45ml/2–3 tbsp sea salt and half the lemon juice, then top up with boiling water to cover the lemon wedges. Seal the jars and leave to stand for 2–4 weeks before using.

3 To use, rinse the preserved lemons well to remove some of the salty flavour, then pull off and discard the flesh. Cut the lemon rind into strips or leave in chunks and use as desired.

Makes about 2 jars

INGREDIENTS

10 unwaxed lemons

about 200ml/7fl oz/scant 1 cup fresh lemon juice or a combination of fresh and preserved juice

boiling water

sea salt

COOK'S TIP

The salty, well-flavoured juice that is used to preserve the lemons can be used to flavour salad dressings or added to hot sauces.

1 Wash the lemons well and cut each into six to eight wedges. Press a generous amount of salt on to the cut surface of each wedge.

pickled limes

This hot, pungent pickle comes from the Punjab in India. Salting softens the rind and intensifies the flavour of the limes, while they mature in the first month or two of storage. Pickled limes are extremely salty so are best served with slightly under-seasoned dishes.

Makes about 1kg/2¼lb

INGREDIENTS

1kg/2¼lb unwaxed limes

75g/3oz/⅓ cup salt

seeds from 6 green cardamom pods

6 whole cloves

5ml/1 tsp cumin seeds

4 fresh red chillies, seeded and sliced

5cm/2in piece fresh root ginger, peeled and finely shredded

450g/1lb/2¼ cups preserving or granulated sugar

1 Put the limes in a large bowl and pour over cold water to cover. Leave to soak for 8 hours, or overnight, if preferred.

2 The next day, remove the limes from the water. Using a sharp knife, cut each lime in half from end to end, then cut each half into 5mm/¼in-thick slices.

3 Place the lime slices in the bowl, sprinkling the salt between the layers. Cover and leave to stand for a further 8 hours.

4 Drain the limes, catching the juices in a preserving pan. Crush the cardamom seeds with the cumin seeds. Add to the pan with the chillies, ginger and sugar. Bring to the boil, stirring until the sugar dissolves. Simmer for 2 minutes and leave to cool.

5 Mix the limes in the syrup. Pack into sterilized jars, cover and seal. Store in a cool, dark place for at least 1 month before eating. Use within 1 year.

striped spiced oranges

These delightful sweet-sour spiced orange slices have a wonderfully warming flavour and look very pretty. Serve them with baked ham, rich terrines and gamey pâtés. They are also delicious with roasted red peppers and grilled halloumi cheese.

Makes about 1.2kg/2½lb

INGREDIENTS

6 small or medium oranges

750ml/1¼ pints/3 cups white wine vinegar

900g/2lb/4½ cups preserving or granulated sugar

7.5cm/3in cinnamon stick

5ml/1 tsp whole allspice

8 whole cloves

45ml/3 tbsp brandy (optional)

COOK'S TIP

These preserved oranges, with their bright colour and warming flavour, make them a perfect accompaniment during the festive season – delicious with leftover turkey or wafer thin slices of festive ham.

1 Scrub the oranges well, then cut strips of rind from each one using a canelle knife (zester) to achieve a striped effect. Reserve the strips of rind.

2 Using a sharp knife, cut the oranges across into slices slightly thicker than 5mm/¼in. Remove and discard any pips (seeds).

3 Put the orange slices into a preserving pan and pour over just enough cold water to cover the fruit. Bring to the boil, then reduce the heat and simmer gently for about 5 minutes, or until the oranges are tender. Using a slotted spoon, transfer the orange slices to a large bowl and discard the cooking liquid.

4 Put the vinegar and sugar in the cleaned pan. Tie the cinnamon, whole allspice and orange rind together in muslin (cheesecloth) and add to the pan. Slowly bring to the boil, stirring, until the sugar has dissolved. Simmer for 1 minute.

5 Return the oranges slices to the pan and cook gently for about 30 minutes, or until the rind is translucent and the orange slices look glazed. Remove from the heat and discard the spice bag.

6 Using a slotted spoon, transfer the orange slices to hot sterilized jars, adding the cloves between the layers. Bring the syrup to a rapid boil and boil for about 10 minutes, or until slightly thickened.

7 Allow the syrup to cool for a few minutes, then stir in the brandy, if using. Pour the syrup into the jars, making sure that the fruit is completely immersed. Gently tap the jars on the work surface to release any air bubbles, then cover and seal. Store for at least 2 weeks before using. Use within 6 months.

pickled plums

This preserve is popular in Central Europe and works well for all varieties of plums, from small wild bullaces and astringent damsons to the more delicately flavoured yellow or red-flushed mirabelle. Plums soften easily, so make sure that you choose very firm fruit.

Makes about 900g/2lb

INGREDIENTS

900g/2lb firm plums

150ml/¼ pint/⅔ cup clear apple juice

450ml/¾ pint/scant 2 cups cider vinegar

2.5ml/½ tsp salt

8 allspice berries

2.5cm/1in piece fresh root ginger, peeled and cut into matchstick strips

4 bay leaves

675g/1½lb/scant 3½ cups preserving or granulated sugar

VARIATION

Juniper berries can be used instead of the allspice berries.

1 Wash the plums, then prick them once or twice using a wooden cocktail stick (toothpick). Put the apple juice, vinegar, salt, allspice berries, ginger and bay leaves in a preserving pan.

2 Add the plums to the pan and slowly bring to the boil. Reduce the heat and simmer gently for 10 minutes, or until the plums are just tender. Remove the plums with a slotted spoon and pack them into hot sterilized jars.

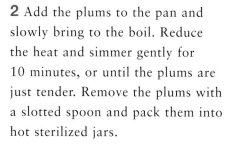

3 Add the sugar to the pan and stir over a low heat until dissolved. Boil steadily for 10 minutes, or until the mixture is syrupy.

4 Leave the syrup to cool for a few minutes, then pour over the plums. Cover and seal. Store for at least 1 month before using and use within 1 year of making.

italian mustard fruit pickles

This traditional and popular Italian preserve is made with late summer and autumn fruits, and then left to mature in time for Christmas when it is served with Italian steamed sausage. The fruits can be mixed together, or arranged in layers in the jars for a stunning effect.

Makes about 1.2kg/2½lb

INGREDIENTS

450ml/¾ pint/scant 2 cups white
  wine vinegar

30ml/2 tbsp mustard seeds

1kg/2¼lb mixed fruit, such as peaches,
  nectarines, apricots, plums, melon,
  figs and cherries

675g/1½lb/scant 3½ cups preserving
  or granulated sugar

VARIATION

If you prefer a slightly less tangy
pickle, use cider vinegar instead of
the white wine vinegar used here.

1 Put the vinegar and mustard seeds in a pan, bring to the boil, then simmer for 5 minutes. Remove from the heat, cover and leave to infuse for 1 hour. Strain the vinegar into a clean pan and discard the mustard seeds.

2 Prepare the fruit. Wash and pat dry the peaches, nectarines, apricots and plums, then stone (pit) and thickly slice or halve. Cut the melon in half, discard the seeds (pips), then slice into 1cm/½in pieces or scoop into balls using a melon baller. Cut the figs into quarters and remove the stalks from the cherries.

3 Add the sugar to the mustard vinegar and heat gently, stirring occasionally, until the sugar has dissolved completely. Bring to the boil, reduce the heat and simmer for 5 minutes, or until syrupy.

4 Add the fruit to the syrup and poach it over a gentle heat for 5–10 minutes. Some fruit will be ready sooner than others, so lift out as soon as each variety is tender, using a slotted spoon.

5 Pack the fruit into hot sterilized jars. Ladle the hot mustard syrup over the fruit. Cover and seal. Allow the pickles to mature for at least 1 month before eating. Use within 6 months.

sweet pickled watermelon rind

This unusual pickle has a slightly aromatic melon flavour and a crunchy texture. It's the perfect way to use up the part of the fruit that is normally discarded.

Makes about 900g/2lb

INGREDIENTS

900g/2lb watermelon rind
  (from 1 large fruit)
50g/2oz/¼ cup salt
900ml/1½ pints/3¾ cups water
450g/1lb/2¼ cups preserving or
  granulated sugar
300ml/½ pint/1¼ cups white wine vinegar
6 whole cloves
7.5cm/3in cinnamon stick

COOK'S TIP

Leave the watermelon rind to mature for at least 4 weeks before eating. This really helps the flavours to develop.

1 Remove the dark green skin from the watermelon rind, leaving a thin layer, no more than 3mm/⅛in thick, of the pink fruit. Cut the rind into slices about 5cm × 5mm/2 × ¼in thick, and place in a large bowl.

2 Dissolve the salt in 600ml/1 pint/ 2½ cups of the water. Pour over the watermelon rind, cover and leave for at least 6 hours or overnight.

3 Drain the watermelon rind and rinse under cold water. Put the rind in a pan and cover with fresh water. Bring the boil, reduce the heat and simmer for 10–15 minutes until just tender. Drain well.

4 Put the sugar, vinegar and remaining water in a clean pan. Tie the cloves and cinnamon in muslin (cheesecloth) and add to the pan. Heat gently, stirring occasionally, until the sugar has dissolved, then bring to the boil and simmer for 10 minutes. Turn off the heat. Add the rind, cover and leave to stand for about 2 hours.

5 Slowly bring the mixture back to the boil, then reduce the heat and simmer gently for 20 minutes, or until the rind has a translucent appearance. Remove and discard the spice bag. Place the rind in hot sterilized jars. Pour over the hot syrup, tapping the jar to release any trapped air. Cover and seal.

blushing pears

As this pickle matures, the fruits absorb the colour of the vinegar, giving them a glorious pink hue. They're especially good served with cold turkey, game pie, well-flavoured cheese or pâté.

Makes about 1.3kg/3lb

INGREDIENTS

1 small lemon

450g/1lb/2¼ cups golden granulated sugar

475ml/16fl oz/2 cups raspberry vinegar

7.5cm/3in cinnamon stick

6 whole cloves

6 allspice berries

150ml/¼ pint/⅔ cup water

900g/2lb firm pears

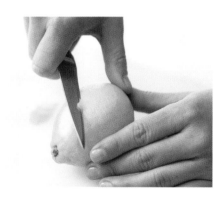

1 Using a sharp knife, thinly pare a few strips of rind from the lemon. Squeeze out 30ml/2 tbsp of the juice and put it in a large pan with the strips of rind.

2 Add the sugar, vinegar, spices and water to the pan. Heat gently, stirring occasionally, until the sugar has completely dissolved, then slowly bring to the boil.

VARIATION

Nectarines and peaches may be pickled using the same method. Blanch and skin the fruits, then halve and stone (pit). Add a strip of orange rind to the syrup instead of lemon rind.

3 Meanwhile, prepare the pears. Peel and halve the pears, then scoop out the cores using a melon baller or small teaspoon. If the pears are very large, cut them into quarters rather than halves.

4 Add the pears to the pan and simmer very gently for about 20 minutes, or until tender and translucent but still whole. Check the pears frequently towards the end of the cooking time. Using a slotted spoon, remove the pears from the pan and pack into hot sterilized jars, adding the spices and strips of lemon rind.

5 Boil the syrup for 5 minutes, or until slightly reduced. Skim off any scum, then ladle the syrup over the pears. Cover and seal. Store for at least 1 month before eating.

relishes

These fabulous condiments can be fresh and quick to prepare or rich and slowly simmered. They usually have bold, striking flavours with a piquant, sharp and spicy taste balanced by sweet and tangy tones. They are perfect for serving with cheese, cold or grilled meats or for jazzing up plain sandwich fillings.

tart tomato relish

Adding lime to this relish gives it a wonderfully tart, tangy flavour and a pleasantly sour after-taste. It is particularly good served with grilled or roast meats such as pork or lamb.

Makes about 500g/1¼lb

INGREDIENTS

2 pieces preserved stem ginger

1 lime

450g/1lb cherry tomatoes

115g/4oz/½ cup muscovado (molasses) sugar

120ml/4fl oz/½ cup white wine vinegar

5ml/1 tsp salt

VARIATION

Use chopped tomatoes in place of the cherry tomatoes, if you prefer.

1 Coarsely chop the preserved stem ginger. Slice the lime thinly, including the rind, then chop the slices into small pieces.

2 Place the cherry tomatoes, sugar, vinegar, salt, ginger and lime in a large heavy pan.

3 Bring the mixture to the boil, stirring until the sugar dissolves, then simmer rapidly for about 45 minutes. Stir frequently until the liquid has evaporated and the relish is thick and pulpy.

4 Leave the relish to cool for about 5 minutes, then spoon into sterilized jars. Leave to cool, then cover and store in the refrigerator for up to 1 month.

COOK'S TIP

There is always discussion between preserving enthusiasts as to the best choice of covering for chutneys and pickles. While cellophane covers are vinegarproof, they are difficult to secure for a good airtight seal, and not very good once opened. Screw-top lids with a plastic coating inside are best: put them on as soon as the piping hot preserve is potted and they will provide a hygienic, air-tight seal. New lids can be purchased for standard-size glass jars.

malay mixed vegetable relish

This traditional, full-flavoured relish, with its crunchy texture and spicy kick, is known as acar kuning *in Malaysia. It is served in very generous portions, almost like a side salad.*

Makes about 900g/2lb

INGREDIENTS

12 small pickling (pearl) onions, quartered

225g/8oz French (green) beans, cut into 2.5cm/1in lengths

225g/8oz carrots, cut into 2.5cm/1in long thin sticks

225g/8oz cauliflower, cut into small florets

5ml/1 tsp mustard powder

5ml/1 tsp salt

10ml/2 tsp granulated sugar

60ml/4 tbsp sesame seeds

For the spice paste

2 shallots, finely chopped

2 garlic cloves, crushed

2 fresh green chillies, seeded and finely chopped

115g/4oz/1 cup dry-roasted peanuts

5ml/1 tsp turmeric

5ml/1 tsp chilli powder

60ml/4 tbsp distilled (white) vinegar

30ml/2 tbsp vegetable oil

175ml/6fl oz/¾ cup boiling water

1 Make the spice paste. Put the shallots, garlic, chillies, peanuts, turmeric, chilli powder, vinegar and oil in a food processor or blender and process to a fairly smooth paste.

2 Transfer the mixture to a large heavy pan and slowly bring to the boil. Reduce the heat and simmer gently for 2 minutes, stirring all the time. Gradually stir in the water and simmer the mixture for a further 3 minutes.

3 Add the onions to the pan, cover and simmer for 5 minutes, then add the beans and carrots. Cover the pan again and cook for a further 3 minutes.

4 Finally, add the cauliflower, mustard, salt and sugar to the pan and simmer, uncovered, for about 5 minutes, or until the vegetables are tender and have absorbed most of the sauce. Remove the pan from the heat and set aside to cool for a few minutes.

5 Meanwhile, toast the sesame seeds in a non-stick pan over a medium heat until golden, stirring frequently. Stir the seeds into the vegetable mixture.

6 Spoon the relish into warmed sterilized jars, cover and seal. Leave until completely cold, then store in the refrigerator.

COOK'S TIP

The relish can be served immediately and should be used within 4 weeks.

carrot and almond relish

This is a Middle Eastern classic, usually made with long fine strands of carrot, available from many supermarkets. Alternatively, grate large carrots lengthways on a medium grater.

Makes about 675g/1½lb

INGREDIENTS

15ml/1 tbsp coriander seeds

500g/1¼lb carrots, grated

50g/2oz fresh root ginger,
  finely shredded

200g/7oz/1 cup caster (superfine) sugar

finely grated rind and juice
  of 1 lemon

120ml/4fl oz/½ cup white wine vinegar

75ml/5 tbsp water

30ml/2 tbsp clear honey

7.5ml/1½ tsp salt

50g/2oz/½ cup flaked (sliced) almonds

2 Put the lemon juice, vinegar, water, honey and salt in a jug (pitcher) and stir until the salt has dissolved. Pour over the carrot mixture. Mix well, cover and leave in the refrigerator for 4 hours.

3 Transfer the chilled mixture to a preserving pan. Slowly bring to the boil, then reduce the heat and simmer for 15 minutes until the carrots and ginger are tender.

4 Increase the heat and boil for 15 minutes, or until most of the liquid has evaporated and the mixture is thick. Stir frequently towards the end of the cooking time to prevent the mixture from sticking to the pan.

5 Put the almonds in a frying pan and toast over a low heat until just beginning to colour. Gently stir into the relish, taking care not to break the almonds.

1 Crush the coriander seeds using a mortar and pestle. Put them in a bowl with the carrots, ginger, sugar and lemon rind and mix together well to combine.

6 Spoon the relish into warmed sterilized jars, cover and seal. Leave for at least 1 month and use within 18 months. Once opened, store in the refrigerator.

nectarine relish

This sweet and tangy fruit relish goes very well with hot roast meats such as pork and game birds such as guinea fowl and pheasant. Make it while nectarines are plentiful and keep tightly covered in the refrigerator to serve for Christmas, or even to give as a seasonal gift.

Makes about 450g/1lb

INGREDIENTS

45ml/3 tbsp olive oil

2 Spanish onions, thinly sliced

1 fresh green chilli, seeded and finely chopped

5ml/1 tsp finely chopped fresh rosemary

2 bay leaves

450g/1lb nectarines, stoned (pitted) and cut into chunks

150g/5oz/1 cup raisins

10ml/2 tsp crushed coriander seeds

350g/12oz/1½ cups demerara (raw) sugar

200ml/7fl oz/scant 1 cup red wine vinegar

1 Heat the oil in a large pan. Add the onions, chilli, rosemary and bay leaves. Cook, stirring frequently, for about 15 minutes, or until the onions are soft.

COOK'S TIP

Pots of this relish make a lovely gift. Store it in pretty jars and add a colourful label identifying the relish, and reminding the recipient that it should be stored in the refrigerator, and when it should be used by.

2 Add the nectarines, raisins, coriander seeds, sugar and vinegar to the pan, then slowly bring to the boil, stirring frequently.

3 Reduce the heat under the pan and simmer gently for 1 hour, or until the relish is thick and sticky. Stir occasionally during cooking, and more frequently towards the end of cooking time to prevent the relish sticking to the pan.

4 Spoon the relish into warmed, sterilized jars and seal. Leave the jars to cool completely, then store in the refrigerator. The relish will keep well in the refrigerator for up to 5 months.

savoury jellies

Although many of the jellies in this chapter contain sugar, they are all prepared as a condiment to serve with savoury foods such as meat, fish or cheese. Soft or firmly set, these interesting jellies are made from fruits and vegetables and usually have a tangy, sweet-and-sour taste. Many are flavoured with zesty citrus fruits and are spiked with herbs and spices to produce wonderful aromatic flavours. They really are a true gourmet treat – enjoy!

lemon grass and ginger jelly

This aromatic jelly is delicious with Asian-style roast meat and poultry such as Chinese crispy duck. It is also the perfect foil for rich fish, especially cold smoked trout or mackerel.

2 Put the chopped lemon grass in a preserving pan and pour over the water. Add the lemons and ginger. Bring to the boil, then reduce the heat, cover and simmer for 1 hour, or until the lemons are pulpy.

3 Pour the fruit and juices into a sterilized jelly bag suspended over a large bowl. Leave to drain for at least 3 hours, or until the juice stops dripping.

4 Measure the juice into the cleaned preserving pan, adding 450g/1lb/2¼ cups sugar for every 600ml/1 pint/2½ cups juice.

5 Heat the mixture gently, stirring occasionally, until the sugar has dissolved completely. Boil rapidly for about 10 minutes until the jelly reaches setting point (105°C/ 220°F). Remove from the heat.

6 Skim any scum off the surface using a slotted spoon, then pour the jelly into warmed sterilized jars, cover and seal. Store in a cool, dark place and use within 1 year. Once opened, keep in the refrigerator. Eat within 3 months.

Makes about 900g/2lb

INGREDIENTS

2 lemon grass stalks

1.5 litres/2½ pints/6¼ cups water

1.3kg/3lb lemons, washed and cut into small pieces

50g/2oz fresh root ginger, unpeeled, thinly sliced

about 450g/1lb/2¼ cups preserving or granulated sugar

1 Using a rolling pin, bruise the lemon grass, then chop roughly.

roasted red pepper and chilli jelly

The hint of chilli in this glowing red jelly makes it ideal for spicing up hot or cold roast meat, sausages or hamburgers. The jelly is also good stirred into sauces or used as a glaze for poultry.

Makes about 900g/2lb

INGREDIENTS

8 red (bell) peppers, quartered
  and seeded

4 fresh red chillies, halved and seeded

1 onion, roughly chopped

2 garlic cloves, roughly chopped

250ml/8fl oz/1 cup water

250ml/8fl oz/1 cup white wine vinegar

7.5ml/1½ tsp salt

450g/1lb/2¼ cups preserving
  or granulated sugar

25ml/1½ tbsp powdered pectin

4 Scrape the purée into a large stainless steel pan, then stir in the white wine vinegar and salt.

5 In a bowl, combine the sugar and pectin, then stir it into the pepper mixture. Heat gently, stirring, until the sugar and pectin have dissolved completely, then bring to a rolling boil. Cook the jelly, stirring frequently, for exactly 4 minutes, then remove the pan from the heat.

6 Pour the jelly into warmed, sterilized jars. Leave to cool and set, then cover, label and store.

1 Arrange the peppers, skin side up, on a rack in a grill (broiling) pan and grill (broil) until the skins blister and blacken.

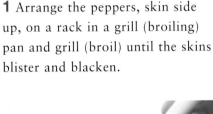

2 Put the peppers in a polythene bag until they are cool enough to handle, then remove the skins.

3 Put the skinned peppers, chillies, onion, garlic and water in a food processor or blender and process to a purée. Press the purée through a nylon sieve set over a bowl, pressing hard with a wooden spoon, to extract as much juice as possible. There should be about 750ml/1¼ pints/3 cups.

tomato and herb jelly

This dark golden jelly is delicious served with roast and grilled meats, especially lamb. It is also great for enlivening tomato-based pasta sauces: stirring a couple of teaspoons of the jelly into sauces helps to heighten their flavour and counteract acidity.

Makes about 1.3kg/3lb

INGREDIENTS

1.8kg/4lb tomatoes

2 lemons

2 bay leaves

300ml/½ pint/1¼ cups cold water

250ml/8fl oz/1 cup malt vinegar

bunch of fresh herbs such as rosemary, thyme, parsley and mint, plus a few extra sprigs for the jars

about 900g/2lb/4½ cups preserving or granulated sugar

COOK'S TIP

Once you have opened a jar of this jelly, store it in the refrigerator and use within 3 months.

1 Wash the tomatoes and lemons well, then cut the tomatoes into quarters and the lemons into small pieces. Put the chopped tomatoes and lemons in a large heavy pan with the bay leaves and pour over the water and vinegar.

2 Add the herbs, either one herb or a mixture if preferred. (If you are using pungent woody herbs such as rosemary and thyme, use about six sprigs; if you are using milder leafy herbs such as parsley or mint, add about 12 large sprigs.)

3 Bring the mixture to the boil, then reduce the heat. Cover the pan with a lid and simmer for about 40 minutes, or until the tomatoes are very soft.

4 Pour the tomato mixture and all the juices into a sterilized jelly bag suspended over a large bowl. Leave to drain for about 3 hours, or until the juices stop dripping.

5 Measure the juice into the cleaned pan, adding 450g/1lb/ 2¼ cups sugar for every 600ml/ 1 pint/2½ cups juice. Heat gently, stirring, until the sugar dissolves. Boil rapidly for 10 minutes, to setting point (105°C/220°F), then remove from the heat. Skim off any scum.

6 Leave the jelly for a few minutes until a skin forms. Place a herb sprig in each warmed sterilized jar, then pour in the jelly. Cover and seal when cold. Store in a cool, dark place and use within 1 year.

quince and rosemary jelly

The amount of water needed for this jelly varies according to the ripeness of the fruit. For a good set, hard under-ripe quinces should be used as they contain the most pectin. If the fruit is soft and ripe, add a little lemon juice along with the water.

Makes about 900g/2lb

INGREDIENTS

900g/2lb quinces, cut into small pieces, with bruised parts removed

900ml–1.2 litres/1½–2 pints/ 3¾–5 cups water

lemon juice (optional)

4 large sprigs of fresh rosemary

about 900g/2lb/4½ cups preserving or granulated sugar

1 Put the chopped quinces in a large heavy pan with the water, using the smaller volume if the fruit is ripe and the larger volume plus lemon juice if it is hard.

2 Reserve a few small sprigs of rosemary, then add the rest to the pan. Bring to the boil, reduce the heat, cover with a lid and simmer gently until the fruit becomes pulpy.

3 Remove and discard all the rosemary sprigs. (Don't worry about any tiny leaves that have fallen off during cooking). Pour the fruit and juices into a sterilized jelly bag suspended over a large bowl. Leave for 3 hours, or until the juices stop dripping.

4 Measure the drained juice into the cleaned pan, adding 450g/1lb/ 2¼ cups sugar for every 600ml/ 1 pint/2½ cups juice.

5 Heat the mixture gently over a low heat, stirring occasionally, until the sugar has dissolved completely. Bring to the boil, then boil rapidly for about 10 minutes until the jelly reaches setting point (105°C/220°F). Remove the pan from the heat.

6 Skim any scum from the surface using a slotted spoon, then leave the jelly to cool for a few minutes until a thin skin begins to form on the surface.

7 Place a sprig of rosemary in each warmed sterilized jar, then pour in the jelly. Cover and seal when cold. Store in a cool, dark place and use within 1 year. Once the jelly is opened, keep it in the refrigerator and use within 3 months.

minted gooseberry jelly

This classic, tart jelly is an ideal complement to roast lamb. Rather surprisingly, the gooseberry juice takes on a pinkish tinge during cooking so does not produce a green jelly as one would expect.

Makes about 1.2kg/2½lb

INGREDIENTS

1.3kg/3lb/12 cups gooseberries

1 bunch fresh mint

750ml/1¼ pints/3 cups cold water

400ml/14fl oz/1⅔ cups white wine vinegar

about 900g/2lb/4½ cups preserving or
  granulated sugar

45ml/3 tbsp chopped fresh mint

1 Place the gooseberries, mint and water in a preserving pan. Bring to the boil, reduce the heat, cover and simmer for about 30 minutes, until the gooseberries are soft. Add the vinegar and simmer uncovered for a further 10 minutes.

2 Pour the fruit and juices into a sterilized jelly bag suspended over a large bowl. Leave to drain for at least 3 hours, or until the juices stop dripping, then measure the strained juices back into the cleaned preserving pan.

3 Add 450g/1lb/2½ cups sugar for every 600ml/1 pint/2½ cups juice, then heat gently, stirring, until the sugar has dissolved. Bring to the boil and cook for 15 minutes, or to setting point (105°C/220°F). Remove the pan from the heat.

4 Skim any scum from the surface. Leave to cool until a thin skin forms, then stir in the mint.

5 Pour the jelly into warmed sterilized jars, cover and seal. Store and use within 1 year. Once opened, store in the refrigerator and eat within 3 months.

plum and apple jelly

Use dark red cooking plums, damsons or wild plums such as bullaces to offset the sweetness of this deep-coloured jelly. Its flavour complements rich roast meats such as lamb and pork.

Makes about 1.3kg/3lb

INGREDIENTS

900g/2lb plums

450g/1lb tart cooking apples

150ml/¼ pint/⅔ cup cider vinegar

750ml/1¼ pints/3 cups water

about 675g/1½lb/scant 3½ cups
  preserving or granulated sugar

COOK'S TIP

This jelly can be stored for up to 2 years. However, once opened, it should be stored in the refrigerator and eaten within 3 months.

1 Cut the plums in half along the crease, twist the two halves apart, then remove the stones (pits) and roughly chop the flesh. Chop the apples, including the cores and skins. Put the fruit in a large heavy pan with the vinegar and water.

2 Bring the mixture to the boil, reduce the heat, cover and simmer for 30 minutes or until the fruit is soft and pulpy.

3 Pour the fruit and juices into a sterilized jelly bag suspended over a large bowl. Leave to drain for at least 3 hours, or until the fruit juices stop dripping.

4 Measure the juice into the cleaned pan, adding 450g/1lb/ 2¼ cups sugar for every 600ml/ 1 pint/2½ cups juice.

5 Bring the mixture to the boil, stirring occasionally, until the sugar has dissolved, then boil rapidly for about 10 minutes, or until the jelly reaches setting point (105°C/220°F). Remove the pan from the heat.

6 Skim any scum from from the surface, then pour the jelly into warmed sterilized jars. Cover and seal while hot. Store in a cool, dark place and use within 2 years.

blackberry and sloe gin jelly

Although they have a wonderful flavour, blackberries are full of pips, so turning them into a deep-coloured jelly is a good way to make the most of this full-flavoured hedgerow harvest. This preserve is delicious served with richly flavoured roast meats such as lamb.

Makes about 1.3kg/3lb

INGREDIENTS

450g/1lb sloes (black plums)
600ml/1 pint/2½ cups cold water
1.8kg/4lb/16 cups blackberries
juice of 1 lemon
about 900g/2lb/4½ cups preserving
   or granulated sugar
45ml/3 tbsp gin

VARIATION

Sloes are much harder to come by than blackberries and you will usually need to find them growing in the wild. If you can't find sloes, use extra blackberries in their place.

1 Wash the sloes and prick with a fine skewer. Put them in a large heavy pan with the water and bring to the boil. Reduce the heat, cover and simmer for 5 minutes.

2 Briefly rinse the blackberries in cold water and add them to the pan with the lemon juice.

3 Bring the fruit mixture back to a simmer and cook gently for about 20 minutes, or until the sloes are tender and the blackberries very soft, stirring once or twice.

4 Pour the fruit and juices into a sterilized jelly bag suspended over a large bowl. Leave to drain for at least 4 hours or overnight, until the juices have stopped dripping.

5 Measure the fruit juice into the cleaned preserving pan, adding 450g/1lb/2¼ cups sugar for every 600ml/1 pint/2½ cups juice.

6 Heat the mixture gently, stirring occasionally, until the sugar has dissolved completely. Bring to the boil, then boil rapidly for about 10 minutes until the jelly reaches setting point (105°C/220°F). Remove the pan from the heat.

7 Skim off any scum from the surface of the jelly using a slotted spoon, then stir in the gin.

8 Pour the jelly into warmed sterilized jars, cover and seal. Store in a cool, dark place and use within 2 years. Once opened, keep the jelly in the refrigerator and eat within 3 months.

COOK'S TIP

Sloes bring a good level of pectin to the jelly. If all blackberries are used without sloes, select some under-ripe fruit and use preserving sugar with added pectin for a good set.

guava jelly

Fragrant guava makes an aromatic, pale rust-coloured jelly with a soft set and a slightly sweet-sour flavour that is enhanced by lime juice. Guava jelly goes well with goat's cheese.

Makes about 900g/2lb

INGREDIENTS

900g/2lb guavas
juice of 2–3 limes
about 600ml/1 pint/2½ cups cold water
about 500g/1¼lb/2½ cups preserving
  or granulated sugar

1 Thinly peel and halve the guavas. Using a spoon, scoop out the seeds (pips) from the centre of the fruit and discard them.

2 Place halved guavas in a large heavy pan with 15ml/1 tbsp lime juice and the water – there should be just enough to cover the fruit. Bring the mixture to the boil, then reduce the heat, cover with a lid and simmer for 30 minutes, or until the fruit is tender.

3 Pour the fruit and juices into a sterilized jelly bag suspended over a large bowl. Leave to drain for at least 3 hours.

COOK'S TIP

Do not be tempted to squeeze the jelly bag while the fruit juices are draining from it; this will result in a cloudy jelly.

4 Measure the juice into the cleaned preserving pan, adding 400g/14oz/2 cups sugar and 15ml/ 1 tbsp lime juice for every 600ml/ 1 pint/2½ cups guava juice.

5 Heat gently, stirring occasionally, until the sugar has dissolved. Boil rapidly for about 10 minutes. When the jelly reaches setting point, remove the pan from the heat.

6 Skim any scum from the surface of the jelly using a slotted spoon, then pour the jelly into warmed sterilized jars. Cover and seal.

7 Store the jelly in a cool, dark place and use within 1 year. Once opened, keep in the refrigerator and eat within 3 months.

mint sauce

In England, mint sauce is the traditional and inseparable accompaniment to roast lamb. Its fresh, tart, astringent flavour is the perfect foil to rich, strongly flavoured lamb. It is extremely simple to make and is infinitely preferable to the ready-made varieties.

Makes about 250ml/8fl oz/1cup

INGREDIENTS

1 large bunch mint
105ml/7 tbsp boiling water
150ml/¼ pint/⅔ cup wine vinegar
30ml/2 tbsp granulated sugar

COOK'S TIP

To make a quick and speedy Indian raita for serving with crispy popadoms, simply stir a little mint sauce into a small bowl of natural (US plain) yogurt. Serve the raita alongside a bowl of tangy mango chutney.

1 Using a sharp knife, chop the mint very finely and place it in a 600ml/1 pint/2½ cup jug (pitcher). Pour the boiling water over the mint and leave to infuse for about 10 minutes.

2 When the mint infusion has cooled and is lukewarm, stir in the wine vinegar and sugar. Continue stirring (but do not mash up the mint leaves) until the sugar has dissolved completely.

3 Pour the mint sauce into a sterilized bottle or jar, seal and store in the refrigerator.

COOK'S TIP

This mint sauce can keep for up to 6 months stored in the refrigerator, but is best used within 3 weeks.

traditional horseradish sauce

Fiery, peppery horseradish sauce is without doubt the essential accompaniment to roast beef and is also delicious served with smoked salmon. Horseradish, like chillies, is a powerful ingredient so you should take care when handling it and wash your hands straight afterwards.

Makes about 200ml/7fl oz/scant 1 cup

INGREDIENTS

45ml/3 tbsp freshly grated
  horseradish root
15ml/1 tbsp white wine vinegar
5ml/1 tsp granulated sugar
pinch of salt
150ml/¼ pint/⅔ cup thick double
  (heavy) cream, for serving

COOK'S TIP

To counteract the potent fumes of the horseradish, keep the root submerged in water while you chop and peel it. Use a food procssor to do the fine chopping or grating, and avert your head when removing the lid.

1 Place the grated horseradish in a bowl, then add the white wine vinegar, granulated sugar and just a pinch of salt.

2 Stir the ingredients together until thoroughly combined.

3 Pour the mixture into a sterilized jar. It will keep in the refrigerator for up to 6 months.

4 A few hours before you intend to serve the sauce, stir the cream into the horseradish and leave to infuse.

tomato ketchup

Sweet, tangy, spicy tomato ketchup is perfect for serving with barbecued or grilled burgers and sausages. This home-made variety is so much better than store-bought tomato ketchup.

2 Tie the onion with the allspice, peppercorns, rosemary and ginger into a double layer of muslin (cheesecloth) and add to the pan. Chop the celery, plus the leaves, and add to the pan with the sugar, raspberry vinegar, garlic and salt.

3 Bring the mixture to the boil over a fairly high heat, stirring occasionally. Reduce the heat and simmer for 1½–2 hours, stirring regularly, until reduced by half. Purée the mixture in a food processor, then return to the pan, bring to the boil and simmer for 15 minutes. Bottle in clean, sterilized jars and store in the refrigerator. Use within 2 weeks.

Makes about 1.3kg/3lb

INGREDIENTS

2.25kg/5lb very ripe tomatoes

1 onion

6 cloves

4 allspice berries

6 black peppercorns

1 fresh rosemary sprig

25g/1oz fresh root ginger, sliced

1 celery heart

30ml/2 tbsp soft light brown sugar

65ml/4½ tbsp raspberry vinegar

3 garlic cloves, peeled

15ml/1 tbsp salt

1 Carefully peel and seed the ripe tomatoes, then chop and place in a large pan. Peel the onion, leaving the tip and root intact and stud it with the cloves.

barbecue sauce

As well as enlivening burgers and other food cooked on the barbecue, this sauce is also good for all manner of grilled meats and savoury pastries.

Makes about 900ml/1½ pints/3¾ cups

INGREDIENTS

30ml/2 tbsp olive oil

1 large onion, chopped

1 garlic clove, crushed

1 fresh red chilli, seeded and sliced

2 celery sticks, sliced

1 large carrot, sliced

1 medium cooking apple, quartered, cored, peeled and chopped

450g/1lb ripe tomatoes, quartered

2.5ml/½ tsp ground ginger

150ml/¼ pint/⅔ cup malt vinegar

1 bay leaf

4 whole cloves

4 black peppercorns

50g/2oz/¼ cup soft light brown sugar

10ml/2 tsp English mustard

2.5ml/½ tsp salt

4 Put the bay leaf, cloves and peppercorns on a square of muslin (cheesecloth) and tie into a bag with fine string. Add to the pan and bring to the boil. Reduce the heat, cover and simmer for about 45 minutes, stirring occasionally.

5 Add the sugar, mustard and salt to the pan and stir until the sugar dissolves. Simmer for 5 minutes. Leave to cool for 10 minutes, then remove the bag and discard.

6 Press the mixture through a sieve and return to the cleaned pan. Simmer for 10 minutes, or until thickened. Adjust the seasoning.

7 Pour the sauce into hot sterilized bottles or jars, then seal. Heat process, cool and, if using cork-topped bottles, dip the corks in wax. Store in a cool, dark place and use within 1 year. Once opened, store in the refrigerator and use within 2 months.

1 Heat the oil in a large heavy pan. Add the onion and cook over a low heat for 5 minutes.

2 Stir in the garlic, chilli, celery and carrot into the onions and cook for 5 minutes, stirring frequently, until the onion just begins to colour.

3 Add the apple, tomatoes, ground ginger and malt vinegar to the pan and stir to combine.

roasted red pepper and chilli ketchup

Roasting the peppers gives this ketchup a richer, smoky flavour. You can add fewer or more chillies according to taste. Once opened, store in the refrigerator and use within 3 months.

Makes about 600ml/1 pint/2½ cups

INGREDIENTS

900g/2lb red (bell) peppers

225g/8oz shallots

1 tart cooking apple, quartered, cored and roughly chopped

4 fresh red chillies, seeded and chopped

1 large sprig each thyme and parsley

1 bay leaf

5ml/1 tsp coriander seeds

5ml/1 tsp black peppercorns

600ml/1 pint/2½ cups water

350ml/12fl oz/1½ cups red wine vinegar

50g/2oz/scant ¼ cup granulated sugar

5ml/1 tsp salt

7.5ml/1½ tsp arrowroot

1 Preheat the grill (broiler). Place the peppers on a baking sheet and grill for 10–12 minutes, turning regularly, until the skins have blackened. Put the peppers in a plastic bag and leave for 5 minutes.

2 When the peppers are cool enough to handle, peel away the skin, then quarter the peppers and remove the seeds. Roughly chop the flesh and place in a large pan.

3 Put the shallots in a bowl, pour over boiling water and leave to stand for 3 minutes. Drain, then rinse under cold water and peel. Chop the shallots and add to the pan with the apple and chillies.

4 Tie the thyme, parsley, bay leaf, coriander and peppercorns together in a square of muslin (cheesecloth).

5 Add the bag of herbs and the water to the pan and bring to the boil. Reduce the heat, cover and simmer for 30 minutes. Leave to cool for 15 minutes, then remove and discard the muslin bag.

6 Purée the mixture in a food processor, then press through a sieve and return the purée to the cleaned pan. Reserve 15ml/1 tbsp of the vinegar and add the rest to the pan with the sugar and salt.

7 Bring to the boil, stirring until the sugar has dissolved, then simmer for 45 minutes, or until the sauce is well reduced. Blend the arrowroot with the reserved vinegar, stir into the sauce, then simmer for a 2–3 minutes, or until slightly thickened.

8 Pour the sauce into hot sterilized bottles, then seal, heat process and store in a cool, dark place and use within 18 months.

aromatic mustard powder

This pungent condiment has the added flavour of herbs and spices and should be served in small quantities with meats and cheese. To serve, simply mix it with a little water.

Makes about 200g/7oz/1⅔ cups

INGREDIENTS

115g/4oz/1 cup mustard powder
25ml/1½ tbsp ground sea salt
5ml/1 tsp dried thyme
5ml/1 tsp dried tarragon
5ml/1 tsp mixed spice (apple
  pie spice)
2.5ml/½ tsp ground black pepper
2.5ml/½ tsp garlic powder (optional)

1 Put the mustard powder and salt in a small bowl and stir together until evenly blended.

2 Add the dried thyme and tarragon to the mustard with the mixed spice, ground black pepper and garlic powder, if using. Stir until thoroughly mixed.

3 Spoon the mustard powder into small clean, dry jars, then seal tightly. Store it in a cool, dark place and use within 6 months. (Although the mustard powder won't go off, the potency of the herbs and spices will fade with age and the final mustard will not have the same lovely, strong flavour.)

4 To serve, combine the mustard powder with an equal amount of cold water 10 minutes before needed. Mix well until smooth.

COOK'S TIPS

• The mustard is best when freshly made, so mix up small quantities as and when you need it.
• To sharpen the flavour when serving the mustard with rich meats, use about a third cider or tarragon vinegar and two-thirds water. It can also be blended with sherry, white or red wine or port; the latter two will give the mustard a darker colour.
• The mustard powder is also great added to sauces and salad dressings to give extra flavour.

moutarde aux fines herbes

This classic, fragrant mustard may be used either as a delicious condiment or for coating meats such as chicken and pork, or oily fish such as mackerel, before cooking. It is also fabulous smeared thinly on cheese on toast for an added bite.

Makes about 300ml/½ pint/1¼ cups

INGREDIENTS

75g/3oz/scant ½ cup white mustard seeds

50g/2oz/¼ cup soft light brown sugar

5ml/1 tsp salt

5ml/1 tsp whole peppercorns

2.5ml/½ tsp ground turmeric

200ml/7fl oz/scant 1 cup distilled malt vinegar

60ml/4 tbsp chopped fresh mixed herbs, such as parsley, sage, thyme and rosemary

COOK'S TIP

Stir a spoonful of this fragrant mustard into creamy savoury sauces and salad dressings to enhance their flavour.

1 Put the mustard seeds, sugar, salt, whole peppercorns and ground turmeric into a food processor or blender and process for about 1 minute, or until the peppercorns are coarsely chopped.

2 Gradually add the vinegar to the mustard mixture, 15ml/1 tbsp at a time, processing well between each addition, then continue processing until a coarse paste forms.

3 Add the chopped fresh herbs to the mustard and mix well, then leave to stand for 10–15 minutes until the mustard thickens slightly.

4 Spoon the mustard into a 300ml/ ½ pint/1¼ cup sterilized jar. Cover the surface of the mustard with a greaseproof (waxed) paper disc, then seal with a screw-top lid or a cork, and label. Store in a cool, dark place.

honey mustard

Delicious home-made mustards mature to make the most aromatic of condiments. This honey mustard is richly flavoured and is wonderful served with meats and cheeses or stirred into sauces and salad dressings to give an extra, peppery bite. The addition of honey gives the mustard a deliciously rounded, full, slightly sweet flavour.

Makes about 500g/1¼lb

INGREDIENTS

225g/8oz/1 cup mustard seeds

15ml/1 tbsp ground cinnamon

2.5ml/½ tsp ground ginger

300ml/½ pint/1¼ cups white wine vinegar

90ml/6 tbsp dark clear honey

COOK'S TIP

Make sure you use well-flavoured clear, runny honey for this recipe. Set (crystallized) honey does not have the right consistency and will not work well.

1 Put the mustard seeds in a bowl with the spices and pour over the vinegar. Stir well to mix, then leave to soak overnight.

2 The next day, put the mustard mixture in a mortar and pound with a pestle, adding the honey very gradually.

3 Continue pounding and mixing until the mustard resembles a stiff paste. If the mixture is too stiff, add a little extra vinegar to achieve the desired consistency.

4 Spoon the mustard into four sterilized jars, seal and label, then store in the refrigerator and use within 4 weeks.

COOK'S TIP

This sweet, spicy mustard is perfect for adding extra flavour to cheese tarts or quiches. Spread a very thin layer of mustard across the base of the pastry case before adding the filling, then bake according to the recipe. The mustard will really complement the cheese, giving a mouth-watering result.

tarragon and champagne mustard

This delicately flavoured mustard is well worth making and goes particularly well with cold chicken, fish and shellfish. Its mild taste enhances these foods perfectly.

Makes about 250g/9oz

INGREDIENTS

30ml/2 tbsp mustard seeds

75ml/5 tbsp champagne vinegar

115g/4oz/1 cup mustard powder

115g/4oz/½ cup soft light brown sugar

2.5ml/½ tsp salt

50ml/3½ tbsp virgin olive oil

60ml/4 tbsp chopped fresh tarragon

COOK'S TIP

Champagne vinegar has a lovely flavour but can sometimes be hard to find. Look in specialist delicatessens and food stores, or large supermarkets that stock a good range of gourmet foods.

1 Put the mustard seeds and vinegar in a bowl and leave to soak overnight.

2 The next day, tip the mustard seeds and vinegar into a food processor and add the mustard powder, sugar and salt.

3 Blend the mustard mixture until smooth, then slowly add the oil while continuing to blend.

4 Tip the mustard into a bowl, stir in the tarragon, then spoon into sterilized jars, seal and store in a cool, dark place.

horseradish mustard

This tangy mustard has a wonderfully creamy, peppery taste and is an excellent accompaniment to cold meats, smoked fish or cheese. It is also fabulous spread thinly inside cold roast beef sandwiches – a great alternative to the traditional horseradish sauce.

Makes about 400g/14oz

INGREDIENTS

25ml/1½ tbsp mustard seeds

250ml/8fl oz/1 cup boiling water

115g/4oz/1 cup mustard powder

115g/4oz/scant ½ cup granulated sugar

120ml/4fl oz/½ cup white wine
 or cider vinegar

50ml/2fl oz/¼ cup olive oil

5ml/1 tsp lemon juice

30ml/2 tbsp horseradish sauce

COOK'S TIP

For the bests results, use home-made horseradish sauce.

1 Put the mustard seeds in a bowl and pour over the boiling water. Set aside and leave to soak for at least 1 hour.

2 Drain the mustard seeds and discard the soaking liquid, then tip the seeds into a food processor or blender.

3 Add the mustard powder, sugar, white wine or cider vinegar, olive oil, lemon juice and horseradish sauce to the mustard seeds in the food processor or blender

4 Process the ingredients into a smooth paste, then spoon the mustard into sterilized jars. Store the mustard in the refrigerator and use within 3 months.

spiced tamarind mustard

Tamarind has a distinctive sweet and sour flavour, a dark brown colour and sticky texture. Combined with spices and ground mustard seeds, it makes a wonderful condiment.

Makes about 200g/7oz

INGREDIENTS

115g/4oz tamarind block

150ml/¼ pint/⅔ cup warm water

50g/2oz/¼ cup yellow mustard seeds

25ml/1½ tbsp black or brown
  mustard seeds

10ml/2 tsp clear honey

pinch of ground cardamom

pinch of salt

COOK'S TIP

The mustard will be ready to eat in 3–4 days. It should be stored in a cool, dark place and used within 4 months.

1 Put the tamarind in a small bowl and pour over the water. Leave to soak for 30 minutes. Mash to a pulp with a fork, then strain through a fine sieve into a bowl.

2 Grind the mustard seeds in a spice mill or coffee grinder and add to the tamarind with the remaining ingredients. Spoon into sterilized jars, cover and seal.

clove-spiced mustard

This spicy mustard is the perfect accompaniment to robust red meats such as sausages and steaks, particularly when they are cooked on the barbecue.

Makes about 300ml/½ pint/1¼ cups

INGREDIENTS

75g/3oz/scant ½ cup white
  mustard seeds

50g/2oz/¼ cup soft light brown sugar

5ml/1 tsp salt

5ml/1 tsp black peppercorns

5ml/1 tsp cloves

5ml/1 tsp turmeric

200ml/7fl oz/scant 1 cup distilled
  malt vinegar

COOK'S TIP

Cloves add a lovely, warming taste to this mustard. Make sure you use whole cloves in this mustard – ground cloves tend to have less flavour.

1 Put all the ingredients except the malt vinegar into a food processor or blender and process. Gradually add the vinegar, 15ml/1 tbsp at a time, processing well between each addition. Continue processing the mustard until it forms a fairly thick, coarse paste.

2 Leave the mustard to stand for 10–15 minutes to thicken slightly. Spoon into a 300ml/½ pint/1¼ cup sterilized jar or several smaller jars, using a funnel. Cover the surface with a greaseproof (waxed) paper disc, then seal with a screw-top lid or a cork, and label.

SHOPPING AND FURTHER INFORMATION

AUSTRALIA

Accoutrement Cook Shops
Good selection of general kitchen
equipment.
118 Queen Corner
Woollahra NSW
Tel: (02) 9362 0151
also at:
611 Military Rd
Mosman NSW
Tel: (02) 9969 1031
and:
808 Pacific Highway
Gordon NSW
Tel: (02) 9418 2992

Bop Discount Kitchenware
Good selection of general kitchen
equipment for delivery anywhere
in Australia.
196 Harris Street
Pyrmont NSW
Tel: (02) 9571 4988
Fax: (02) 9571 5688
Email: sucram@ihug.com.au

Kitchen Centre
Online service offering range of
preserving equipment.
Website: kitchen.centre.net.au

CANADA

Farmer's Market Directory
Comprehensive website offering
a state-by-state directory of
farmer's markets.
Website: chef2chef.net/farmer-
markets/canada

Homecanning.com
Online service offering good range
of preserving equipment.
Bernardin Ltd
120 The East Mall
Toronto ON M8Z 5V5
Fax: (416) 239 4424
Website: www.homecanning.com

NEW ZEALAND

Arthur Holmes Limited
Good selection of glass storage jars
and bottles.
10–30 Horner Street
Newtown
Wellington
Tel: (04) 389 4103
Email: email@arthurholmes.co.nz
Website: www.arthurholmes.co.nz

Crofter Supplies
Mail-order and online ordering
service offering range of preserving
jars and bottles, and other equipment.
PO Box 80 212
Green Bay
Auckland
Tel: (09) 817 2216
Website: www.crofter.co.nz

The Scullery
Mail-order service offering good
range of general kitchen equipment.
391 Victoria Street
Hamilton
Tel: (07) 839 9001
Website: www.shop@thescullery.co.nz

Total Food Equipment Limited
Good range of preserve-making
equipment and accessories.
29 Bower Street
Napier
Tel: (06) 834 4004
Fax: (06) 834 2925
Email: totalfood@xtra.co.nz
Website: www.tfe.co.nz

SOUTH AFRICA

Durbanville Market
Good range of fresh fruits, vegetables
and local produce.
Frederick Street
Durbanville
Cape Town
Tel: (021) 976 9250
Fax: (021) 976 544

Hillcrest Berry Orchards
Good range of fresh berries and fruit;
quick-frozen produce also available.
Banhoek Valley
R310
Stellenbosch
Cape Town
Tel: (021) 885 1629
Fax: (021) 885 1624
Website: www.hillcrestberries.co.za

UNITED KINGDOM

Cucina Direct

Mail-order catalogue service offering good range of preserve-making equipment and accessories. Online ordering available.
PO Box 6611
London SW15 2WG
Tel: 0870 420 4300
Fax: 0870 420 4330
Website: www.cucinadirect.com

Divertimenti

Good range of preserve-making equipment and accessories. Home delivery and online ordering available.
139–141 Fulham Road
London SW3 6SD
Tel: 020 7581 8065
Web site: www.divertimenti.co.uk
and also at:
33–34 Marylebone High Street
London W1U 4PT
Tel: 020 7935 0689

Farmer's Market Directory

Comprehensive website offering a directory of farmers markets.
Website: www.farmersmarket.co.uk

Harrison Smith French Flint Limited

Excellent range of plain and fancy-shaped glass jars.
Rich House
40 Crimscott Street
London SE1 5TE
Tel: 020 7231 6777

John Lewis

Good range of preserve-making equipment and accessories. Stores throughout the United Kingom and online ordering available.
Oxford Street
London W1A 1EX
Tel: 020 7629 7711
General enquiries: 08456 049049
Website: www.johnlewis.com

Lakeland Limited

Good range of preserve-making equipment and accessories. Comprehensive mail-order catalogue, over 20 stores in the United Kingdom and telephone/online ordering system.
Alexandra Buildings
Windermere, Cumbria LA23 1BQ
Tel: 01539 488 100
www.lakelandlimited.com

Wares of Knutsford

Good range of traditional preserving equipment. Online ordering available.
36a Princess Street
Knutsford
Cheshire WA16 6BN
Tel: 01565 751 477
Fax: 01565 754 718
Email: sales@waresofknutsford.co.uk
Website: www.waresofknutsford.co.uk

UNITED STATES

Cash-us.com

Online ordering service offering good range of preserving equipment.
Website: www.cash-us.com/products/cookware/Cooks_tools/canning_tools

Chefs Store

Online service offering range of preserving and general kitchen equipment.
Website: www/chefs-store.com

Farmer's Market Directory

Comprehensive website offering a state-by-state directory of farmer's markets.
Website: chef2chef.net/farmer-markets

Kitchen Krafts

Online service offering good supply of specialty kitchen tools including preserving equipment and glass bottles and jars.
PO Box 442-ORD
Waukon
Iowa 52172
Tel: 1 800 776 0575
Fax: 1 800 850 3093
Email: Info@kitchenkrafts.com
Website: www.kitchenkrafts.com

Village Kitchen

Online service offering good range of glass preserving jars and bottles, and other equipment.
2774 Tarmac Rd
Suite 1
Redding CA 96003
Website: www.villagekitchen.com

INDEX